THE MOLINIST
ANSWER

Reconciling Providence and Human Freedom

TRUETT JAMES BILLUPS

The Molinist Answer:

Reconciling Providence and Human Freedom

By Truett James Billups

All Scripture quotations are from the English Standard Version.

ISBN-13: 978-0-692-04901-3

Cover background: Designed by Kjpargeter / Freepik

Back cover paint splatter: Designed by 0melapics / Freepik

Edits made to pages 4 and 9 in August 2021.

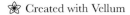 Created with Vellum

Contents

Introduction

Oh, the depth of the riches and wisdom and knowledge of God!
How unsearchable are his judgments and how inscrutable his
ways! (Romans 11:34)

With this thought, Paul closes Romans. And yet, for two
millennia, the project of theology has been to plunge the
depths of God. Theologians scrutinize passages, tease apart
nuances of ancient languages, read books (and sometimes write
them), fly to conferences, ask questions, and ponder deep into
the night. Charles Spurgeon writes,

> The proper study of a Christian is the Godhead. The
> highest science, the loftiest speculation, the mightiest
> philosophy, which can ever engage the attention of a
> child of God, is the name, the nature, the person, the
> work, the doings, and the existence of the great God
> whom he calls his Father....Nothing will so enlarge the
> intellect, nothing so magnify the whole soul of man, as
> a devout, earnest, continued investigation of the great
> subject of the Deity.[1]

However, one of the most troublesome questions of the "great subject of the Deity" is this: How can divine providence be reconciled with human freedom? A river of questions flow from it. If God is all powerful and all good, then why evil? Why is most of humanity condemned to eternal punishment? How did God write the Bible, yet involve human authors? If Christianity is the only way to God, then why is it mostly a Western thing? Theologians spend oceans of ink answering them.

As wide and deep as these questions are, I think Molinism provides some satisfactory answers. It was named after the 16th-century Jesuit counter-reformer Luis de Molina who saw the Reformation as a wholesale denial of human freedom. He desired to offer Luther and the Reformers a theological model that upheld both God's omnipotence and human freedom. Obviously, his ideas didn't catch on with Protestants, but Molinism has enjoyed a quiet revival in recent years due to some high-profile Christians.

Whenever we attempt to plunge the depths of God, we must keep our conclusions tentative. We are attempting to explain mysteries. Nevertheless, I think Molinism should be considered by more Christians. It works surprisingly well to reconcile providence and human freedom and explain several other major areas of theology.

In this book, I will not directly critique other models of divine providence, such as Calvinism, Arminianism, and Open Theism. Given the variety of views, and nuances of views, within each of these models, it seems more effective to critique particular points of beliefs rather than entire sets. I think trying to critique entire sets of beliefs, and all the varieties within them, increases my chances of misrepresenting someone. So, rather than saying, "Calvinists object...," instead I will say, "Some may offer the following objection...," etc. Thus, this paper rarely refers to other models by name. However, this is not meant to dodge critique. Rather, it is meant to offer more accurate answers to specific objections and avoid misrepresenting others.

Section One of this paper starts with some opening arguments. It covers orthodox doctrines of God's attributes and sets up paradoxes that could be seen as troublesome. Section Two describes Molinism and offers answers to the paradoxes. Section Three applies Molinism to six major areas of theology. Section Four responds to common objections.

This is a theology book meant for lay Christians. I will assume orthodox doctrines such as the Trinity, the Incarnation, Christ's bodily resurrection, that Christ is the only way to God, and the authority of the Bible. I'll assume that you, the reader, give assent to the Apostles' Creed and the Nicene Creed. That's our common ground. Also, this book not intended to be a scholarly treatment of Molinism, merely brief and accessible.

The most important point I want readers to understand is this: God does everything out of love. He made humanity out of love. He redeemed humanity out of love. He anguishes over the loss of a single soul. Jesus is the embodiment of that love by being born on this sinful planet, dying on the cross, and resurrecting to offer life to all peoples. "For God so loved the world, that he gave his only Son, that whoever believes in him should not perish but have eternal life" (John 3:16). Nothing is more important to Christianity than proclaiming His love.

Let's begin the ancient project of theology and plunge the depths of God.

Opening Arguments

"**D**efine God and give two examples." It's an old joke—but it's darned accurate. God is unlike any other being imaginable. Ever since the ancient Greeks, the Creator of the universe is traditionally conceived as omniscient, omnipotent, and omnibenevolent. As Christians, we have a longer list, such as personal, volitional, infinite, etc. But these are the three we'll consider. They form our first opening argument.

First, God is omniscient, meaning "all-knowing." Traditionally, this means He knows everything about the universe, such as the amount of atoms in our bodies, the exact distances between stars, and the nuances of our emotions and thoughts. 1 John 3:20 says that God "knows everything," and Jesus says, "Even the hairs of your head are all numbered" (Matthew 10:30). The opening of the apostles' prayer in Acts 1:24 says the Lord knows the "hearts of all." Repeatedly, Jesus demonstrated the ability to know people's thoughts (Matthew 9:4, 12:25; Mark 2:8; Luke 6:8) and warned the Pharisees, "You are those who justify yourselves before men, but God knows your hearts" (Luke 16:15). Other verses supporting this include Acts

15:8; Romans 8:27; 1 Corinthians 4:5; 1 John 3:19-20; and Hebrews 4:12-13.

Psalm 139 speaks beautifully of God's omniscience.

O LORD, you have searched me and known me!
You know when I sit down and when I rise up;
you discern my thoughts from afar.
You search out my path and my lying down
and are acquainted with all my ways.
Even before a word is on my tongue,
behold, O LORD, you know it altogether.
You hem me in, behind and before,
and lay your hand upon me.
Such knowledge is too wonderful for me;
it is high; I cannot attain it. (vv. 1-6)

As verse 4 suggests, God also knows the future. He planned Abraham's offspring (Genesis 15:13-14). God planned Christ's atonement from the beginning of time, as Paul indicates in several passages (Ephesians 1:9-11, 3:9-10; 2 Timothy 1:9-10), as well as Peter (1 Peter 1:10-11, 1:19-20). This also means that, prior to the dawn of time, God knew mankind would fall. Correctly foreknowing the future was a requirement for a prophet of God (Deuteronomy 18:22). The Gospel writers point out that Jesus fulfills a number of Old Testament prophecies (Matthew 1:22; 2:15, 23; 4:14-16; 8:17; 12:17-21; Mark 1:2-4; 9:9-13; Luke 7:18-23, 27; 18:31-33; Acts 2:16-21; 3:18; 4:25-28; 7:52; 8:30-35; 10:43; 15:15-18; John 12:38-41; 19:24, 28, 36). Jesus said that these prophets foreknew Him, by their knowledge received from God (Luke 24:25-27). Jesus is characterized as a prophet who knows the end of time (Matthew 24; Mark 13; Luke 21), and He foretells His death on Calvary (Matthew 20:17-19). Biblical writers typically view God as having foreknowledge of events. Isaiah affirms,

I am God, and there is no other;
I am God, and there is none like me,
declaring the end from the beginning
and from ancient times things not yet done,
saying, 'My counsel shall stand,
and I will accomplish all my purpose,' (46:9-10)

Second, God is omnipotent, meaning "all-powerful." Some might think this means God can do *anything*, such as making round squares or causing Himself to exist and not exist simultaneously or, more famously, create a rock too heavy for Him to lift. This is false, and we'll discuss why later on. Omnipotence, properly defined, refers to *maximal power*. God has more *power* than any other conceivable being.

The opening of Genesis communicates this...well, powerfully. It says, "In the beginning, God created the heavens and the earth." No other being is capable of creating a universe. Also, God is so powerful that He creates using just His words. Genesis exemplifies this with the continual phrase "And God said" (Chapter 1) followed by the creation of an aspect of the universe. In Romans 4:17, Paul says that God "calls into existence the things that do not exist." This phrase affirms not only God's power, but also subtly refers to His aseity, or self-existence. God does not depend on anything for His existence. Rather, He calls things into existence.[2]

Again, the psalms describe this beautifully.

By the word of the LORD the heavens were made,
and by the breath of his mouth all their host.
He gathers the waters of the sea as a heap;
he puts the deeps in storehouses.
Let all the earth fear the LORD;
let all the inhabitants of the world stand in awe of him!
For he spoke, and it came to be;

he commanded, and it stood firm. (33:6-9)

As God incarnate, Jesus demonstrates this same maximal power over creation. He healed people of diseases and disabilities, fed the crowds (Mark 6:30-44), rose others from the dead (John 11:38-44; Mark 5:35-43), calmed the storm (Mark 4:37-41), and finally gave an example of maximal power that rivals the creation of the universe: He rose from the dead. Christ's Incarnation is a big field of doctrine—such as what it means for Christ to empty Himself (Philippians 2:7) and possibly suppress certain aspects of His deity—but that isn't our concern in this paper. Our concern is with the Godhead proper.

As I said, omnipotence refers to *maximal power,* but not the ability to do *anything.* The reason for this qualification is important: God cannot act contrary to His nature. God is the source of logic and reason. As such, He cannot do things that are logically impossible. He cannot make round squares, married bachelors, or make 2+2=3. This is why God cannot sin (Hebrews 6:18), because it is logically incoherent to say that God can commit a sin and be both omnibenevolent and *not* omnibenevolent simultaneously. He cannot create another being that *also* has maximal power and then fall down and worship it, because God cannot be both God and *not* God simultaneously. That's why the old challenge to theism fails: "Can God create a rock too heavy for Him to lift?" The answer is no, He can't. That is asking God to commit a logical impossibility. He cannot be both omnipotent and *not* omnipotent simultaneously. The reason is precisely *because* He has maximal power, not because He doesn't. The challenge itself is logically impossible. It doesn't constitute what it means for God to have maximal power.[3] In *The Problem of Pain* (Chapter 2), C.S. Lewis agrees with this point and argues in favor of God's inability to perform logical impossibilities.

Theological arguments can be made for God's inability to bring about logically impossible things. One comes from Matthew 26 where Jesus prays in Gethsemane just before His crucifixion. In verse 39, He prays, "My Father, if it be possible, let this cup pass from me; nevertheless, not as I will, but as you will." In verse 42, He prays, "My Father, if this cannot pass unless I drink it, your will be done." Jesus affirms that dying on the cross is the only possible way to absolve humanity of sin and rescue them from evil powers. If God can do logically impossible things, then He could simply forgive humanity and Christ would not have to be crucified. However, the crucifixion of Christ is consistent with God's justice. And consistency is the foundation of what it means to be a logical being. If God can do logically impossible things, then He could have rescued humanity some other (less painful) way and Christ's crucifixion on the cross was unnecessary. However, God is bound by logical constraints according to the consistency of His own being, and so the cross was the only possible way to rescue humanity. The necessity of the Atonement implies some sort of logical boundaries to the power of the Godhead. Jesus affirms these boundaries in Luke 24:26 where He rhetorically asks, "Was it not necessary that the Christ should suffer these things and enter into his glory?" It seems reasonable to conclude that Jesus recognizes certain logical boundaries to the Godhead. Omnipotence should be defined in harmony with those boundaries. God is omnipotent, meaning He has *maximal power*, meaning He can do anything logically possible.

Third, God is omnibenevolent, meaning "all-good." Traditionally, this means He cannot sin and always desires what is good. Being omnibenevolent includes loving what is good and showing perfect love toward others. God brought Israel out of slavery in Egypt because of His love (Deuteronomy 7:7-8). We humans were "foolish, disobedient, [and] led astray," but God saved us because of His "goodness and loving kindness" (Titus

3:3-5). Paul says, "But God shows his love for us in that while we were still sinners, Christ died for us" (Romans 5:8). He also says, "But God, being rich in mercy, because of the great love with which he loved us, even when we were dead in our trespasses, made us alive together with Christ" (Ephesians 2:4-5). Then, of course, the classic verse John 3:16: "For God so loved the world, that he gave his only Son, that whoever believes in him should not perish but have eternal life." All over the Bible, God is said to be all-good and all-loving.

A passage worth quoting at length is 1 John 4:7-21.

> Beloved, let us love one another, for love is from God, and whoever loves has been born of God and knows God. Anyone who does not love does not know God, because God is love. In this the love of God was made manifest among us, that God sent his only Son into the world, so that we might live through him. In this is love, not that we have loved God but that he loved us and sent his Son to be the propitiation for our sins. Beloved, if God so loved us, we also ought to love one another. No one has ever seen God; if we love one another, God abides in us and his love is perfected in us.
>
> By this we know that we abide in him and he in us, because he has given us of his Spirit. And we have seen and testify that the Father has sent his Son to be the Savior of the world. Whoever confesses that Jesus is the Son of God, God abides in him, and he in God. So we have come to know and to believe the love that God has for us. God is love, and whoever abides in love abides in God, and God abides in him. By this is love perfected with us, so that we may have confidence for the day of judgment, because as he is so also are we in this world. There is no fear in love, but perfect love casts out fear. For fear has to do with punishment, and whoever fears has not been perfected in love. We love because he first loved us. If anyone says, "I

love God," and hates his brother, he is a liar; for he who does not love his brother whom he has seen cannot love God whom he has not seen. And this commandment we have from him: whoever loves God must also love his brother.

Theologians unanimously agree that God is omnibenevolent. I can think of some who may question God's omniscience or omnipotence, but no theologian questions God's goodness. It seems to be the one attribute of God on which Christians are absolutely unwilling to adjust their views. A challenge to God's omnibenevolence would hit the core of His being. God *has* knowledge and power, but He *is* love.

This flows smoothly into the second opening argument: God desires all peoples to be saved. In 1 Timothy 2:3-4, Paul writes, "God our Savior…desires all people to be saved and to come to the knowledge of the truth." Two chapters later, Paul clarifies what he means by "all" when he writes that God "is the Savior of all people, especially of those who believe" (4:10). Here, Paul teaches that "those who believe" is a subset of "all people." So "all people" literally means "all people." The passages occur in the same book and flow of thought. God genuinely desires literally all people to be saved. Other supporting passages include the following:

- The Lord is not slow to fulfill his promise as some count slowness, but is patient toward you, not wishing that any should perish, but that all should reach repentance. (2 Peter 3:9)
- "So it is not the will of my Father who is in heaven that one of these little ones should perish." (Matthew 18:14)
- He came as a witness, to bear witness about the light, that all might believe through him. (John 1:7)

- For the grace of God has appeared, bringing salvation for all people. (Titus 2:11)
- For the Son of Man came to seek and to save the lost. (Luke 19:20)

This view makes sense of the following passages:

- "If anyone hears my words and does not keep them, I do not judge him; for I did not come to judge the world but to save the world." (John 12:47)
- And we have seen and testify that the Father has sent his Son to be the Savior of the world. (1 John 4:14)
- They said to the woman, "It is no longer because of what you said that we believe, for we have heard for ourselves, and we know that this is indeed the Savior of the world." (John 4:42)
- He is the propitiation for our sins, and not for ours only but also for the sins of the whole world. (1 John 2:2)
- The next day he saw Jesus coming toward him, and said, "Behold, the Lamb of God, who takes away the sin of the world!" (John 1:29)

The classic paradox follows. If God is omnipotent, omniscient, and omnibenevolent, and truly desires all peoples to be saved, then why are so many lost? This is similar to the problem of evil, or suffering.

Some Christians answer that God has a *higher desire*, namely His own glory. God desires all peoples to be saved, but His desire to glorify Himself supersedes it. Many people are eternally separated from Christ because somehow that brings God glory and we are cognitively limited in knowing how or why.

Therefore, everything God does is ultimately for His own glory.

I caution against this for three reasons. My first caution: Placing God's desire for His own glory above His desire to save all peoples doesn't seem to have clear Scriptural support. In fact, Scripture seems to teach that God does everything because of His love for humanity and His desire to save them, rather than a sole desire for His own glory. 1 Peter 1:20-21 seems to answer the question.

> He was chosen before the creation of the world, but was revealed in these last times for your sake. Through him you believe in God, who raised him from the dead and glorified him, and so your faith and hope are in God.

Here, Peter says that Jesus was revealed "for your sake." He also identifies that one's faith and hope is a result of God's glorifying Jesus (v. 21). The Greek conjunction "and so" is hóste, which refers to an *effect* or *result*. If there is a hierarchy of God's desires, then it is this: Firstly, He desires to save all peoples. Secondly, He desires to bring glory to Himself. If God does something to glorify Himself, it is for the ultimate goal of bringing more people into a saving knowledge and relationship with Him.

Most of Scripture attributes God's actions to His love for humanity and His highest desire to save them. Jesus said He came to Earth "to seek and to save the lost" (Luke 19:10), and "the Son of Man came not to be served but to serve" (Mark 10:45). Consider the following passages.

- It was not because you were more in number than any other people that the LORD set his love on you and chose you, for you were the fewest of all peoples, but it is because the LORD loves you and is keeping the oath that he swore to your fathers, that the LORD has brought you out with a mighty hand and redeemed you from the house of slavery, from the hand of Pharaoh king of Egypt. (Deuteronomy 7:7-8)

- But God, being rich in mercy, because of the great love with which he loved us, even when we were dead in our trespasses, made us alive together with Christ—by grace you have been saved.... (Ephesians 2:4-5)

- For we ourselves were once foolish, disobedient, led astray, slaves to various passions and pleasures, passing our days in malice and envy, hated by others and hating one another. But when the goodness and loving kindness of God our Savior appeared, he saved us, not because of works done by us in righteousness, but according to his own mercy, by the washing of regeneration and renewal of the Holy Spirit.... (Titus 3:3-5)

- But God shows his love for us in that while we were still sinners, Christ died for us. (Romans 5:8)

- In him we have redemption through his blood, the forgiveness of our trespasses, according to the riches of his grace, which he lavished upon us, in all wisdom and insight making known to us the mystery of his will, according to his purpose, which he set forth in Christ as a plan for the fullness of time, to unite all things in him, things in heaven and things on earth. (Ephesians 1:7-10)

- Father, I desire that they also, whom you have given me, may be with me where I am, to see my glory that you have given me because you loved me before the foundation of the world. (John 17:24)

Some passages give a strong indication of God's desire to glorify Himself (Isaiah 43:7; Isaiah 48:9-11; 1 Corinthians 10:31; Ephesians 1:11-14; Acts 12:23; 2 Thessalonians 1:9-10; Romans 9:22-24; Romans 9:17; Psalm 106:7-8; Jeremiah 13:11). They could be interpreted as a challenge to the hierarchy of God's desires that I've proposed. However, from my view, none of them actually propose an explicit hierarchy in the same way as Romans 3:21-26. I encourage you to look up these passages and decide how to interpret them in light of God's omnibenevolence.

My second caution: Saying God's higher desire is to glorify Himself seems to challenge His omnibenevolence. If everything He does is ultimately for His own benefit, then is He truly omnibenevolent? Of course, some will say, "God glorifies Himself for *our* benefit," and yet that seems to be backpedalling. It admits that God glorifies Himself *for the higher purpose* of saving humanity. Is God's highest desire to glorify Himself, or save humanity?

My third caution: Saying God's highest desire is to glorify Himself seems to eradicate Him as a moral example. If God is the ultimate example of goodness (omnibenevolence) after which we strive and model our lives, then saying His highest desire is to glorify Himself seems to leave us with no true moral example. We conclude: Because He *is* love, God desires all peoples to be saved.

Some might object that God has a secret, or hidden, will that supersedes God's glory. They might refer to passages like Deuteronomy 29:29, which says, "The secret things belong to the LORD our God, but the things that are revealed belong to us and to our children forever, that we may do all the words of this law." The problem with this objection is that it seems to forget something important: Jesus came to Earth and revealed the will of the Father. Paul says that Christ "[made] known to us the mystery of his will" which is to "unite all things in him, things in heaven and things on earth" (Ephesians 1:9-10). Paul repeats the point in Colossians 1:19, "For in [Jesus] all the fullness of God was pleased to dwell, and through him to reconcile to himself all things, whether on earth or in heaven, making peace by the blood of his cross." This is consistent with God's love for the world (John 3:16), His desire for the salvation of all peoples (1 Timothy 2:3-4), and why He expanded salvation to include the Gentiles (Ephesians 3:9). Jesus says in Revelation, "Behold, I stand at the door and knock. If anyone hears my voice and opens the door, I will come in to him and eat with him, and he with me" (3:20). There are no mysteries with regard to His will—they were revealed to us. God's highest desire is to save all individuals and have a relationship with them, to "unite" with them, to stand at the door of everyone's heart and knock.

Back to the paradox: If God is omniscient, omnipotent, and omnibenevolent, and truly desires all peoples to be saved, then why are so many lost? Our third argument says that something must be hindering His desire, and the most likely candidate is human freedom. In Luke 7:30, "the Pharisees and the lawyers rejected the purpose of God for themselves, not having been baptized by him." In Acts 7:51, Stephen rebukes his accusers, "You stiff-necked people, uncircumcised in heart and ears, you always resist the Holy Spirit. As your fathers did, so do you." James indicates this human responsibility when he urges his readers to "receive with meekness the implanted word, which is able to save your souls" (1:21). In Matthew 7:7 during the Sermon on the Mount, Jesus clearly recognizes his audience's ability to choose (who included all kinds of people, not just His disciples), saying, "Ask, and it will be given to you; seek, and you will find; knock, and it will be opened to you." (See also Deuteronomy 4:29; 30:19.)

Then there is the Parable of the Sower in Mark 4:1-20. In this passage, Jesus recognizes the ability for humans to accept or reject the Gospel based upon the inclination of their hearts. "But those that were sown on the good soil are the ones who hear the word and accept it and bear fruit, thirtyfold and sixtyfold and a hundredfold" (v. 20). Within the same passage, the disciples wonder why Jesus shrouds the Gospel in parables. Jesus answers, "So that 'they [unbelievers] may indeed see but not perceive, and may indeed hear but not understand, lest they should turn and be forgiven" (v. 12). Here, Jesus recognizes the role of human freedom in salvation and accommodates His actions accordingly, choosing to shroud the Gospel in parables rather than state it explicitly. If human freedom plays no role in salvation, then it wouldn't matter if He explicitly stated the Gospel or not.

A good example of human freedom hindering God's desire to save all peoples is Matthew 23:37. Jesus says, "O Jerusalem, Jerusalem, the city that kills the prophets and stones those who are sent to it! How often would I have gathered your children together as a hen gathers her brood under her wings, and you were not willing!" Jesus clearly expresses His desire to gather the people of Jerusalem under the safety of His love, but attributes the failure of that end to human freedom—they were "not willing."

Another Scriptural argument for the existence of human freedom in salvation can be made from Jesus' condemnation of Corazin and Bethsaida.

> Then he began to denounce the cities where most of his mighty works had been done, because they did not repent. "Woe to you, Chorazin! Woe to you, Bethsaida! For if the mighty works done in you had been done in Tyre and Sidon, they would have repented long ago in sackcloth and ashes. But I tell you, it will be more bearable on the day of judgment for Tyre and Sidon than for you. And you, Capernaum, will you be exalted to heaven? You will be

brought down to Hades. For if the mighty works done in you had been done in Sodom, it would have remained until this day. But I tell you that it will be more tolerable on the day of judgment for the land of Sodom than for you." (Matthew 11:20-24)

Molina himself offers a wonderful exposition of this passage.

For if, on the hypothesis that *those very wonders* should have been worked in Tyre and Sidon, the Tyronians and Sidonians would not have been converted unless God had, *in addition*, predetermined to confer on them some *other* assistance, intrinsically efficacious, which was not in fact conferred on them and with which the people of Chorozain [sic] and Bethsaida would have been converted had it likewise been predetermined for them—if this is so, then, I ask, what is it that Christ is reproaching the people of Chorozain [sic] and Bethsaida for?[4]

Here, Molina rightly asks his opponents: If salvation requires that God first stir and move our faculty of choice, then why is Christ condemning Chorazin and Bethsaida? According to this passage, all it should take is to work miracles in their presence, and then the residents should convert. But to say that God must first stir and move our faculty of choice in some way to bring someone to salvation means that Christ is simply condemning them for not being chosen by God. Human freedom must have a place in salvation, or Christ's condemnation of Tyre and Sidon is meaningless.

Origen writes,

Moreover, in order that you might understand that the cause of each person's salvation is to be found not in God's foreknowledge but in that person's intentions and actions, notice that Paul tormented his body and subjected it to servitude because he feared that, after having preached to others, he himself might perhaps become reprobate.[5]

Well-known theologian D. A. Carson identifies nine streams of Scriptural texts affirming human freedom: (1) People face a multitude of divine exhortations and commands, (2) people are said to obey, believe, and choose God, (3) people sin and rebel against God, (4) people's sins are judged by God, (5) people are tested by God, (6) people receive divine rewards, (7) the elect are responsible to respond to God's initiative, (8) prayers are not mere showpieces scripted by God, and (9) God literally pleads with sinners to repent and be saved.[6]

The existence of human freedom in salvation is consistent with our proper definition of omnipotence: God has maximal power, but cannot act contrary to His nature and do logically impossible things. This includes creating causally-determined free agents.[7] Humans can give each other unpleasant choices (such as a thief holding someone at gunpoint), but neither we—nor God—can truly causally-determine a free agent to do something. Ezekiel 18:23 says, "Have I any pleasure in the death of the wicked, declares the Lord God, and not rather that he should turn from his way and live?" The reason many people reject salvation is because they are free agents.

Moving on to our fourth argument, Scripture also clearly teaches that God predestines individuals to come to saving faith and draws them to Himself. Romans 9 provides a firm foundation for this doctrine. There, Paul says that God predestined Isaac and Esau when they were conceived, "though they were not yet born and had done nothing either good or bad— in order that God's purpose of election might continue, not because of works but because of him who calls" (v. 11). Paul anticipates the objection of unfairness by saying, "Is there injustice on God's part? By no means! For he says to Moses, 'I will have mercy on whom I have mercy, and I will have compassion on whom I have compassion.' So that it depends not on human will or exertion, but on God, who has mercy" (vv. 14-16). Here we have a clear statement of individuals being predestined by God's sovereign grace to come to faith, seemingly independent of human freedom. Paul underscores the point by anticipating and answering the objection of unfairness by essentially saying mankind has no right to object to God's sovereign decrees.

Other passages support God's sovereignty in salvation. In John 15:16, Jesus says to His followers, "You did not choose Me but I chose you, and appointed you that you should go and bear fruit and that your fruit should abide...." And in John 6:44, He says, "No one can come to me unless the Father who sent me draws him." In Acts 13, Paul preaches the Gospel in Antioch, and "when the Gentiles heard this, they began rejoicing and glorifying the word of the Lord, and as many as were appointed to eternal life believed" (v. 48). Then, of course, there is the great Chain of Salvation in Romans 8:29-30, which says, "For those whom he foreknew he also predestined to be conformed to the image of his Son, in order that he might be the firstborn among many brothers. And those whom he predestined he also called, and those whom he called he also justified, and those whom he justified he also glorified." These passages clearly teach that God sovereignly chooses individuals to come to saving faith and draws them to Himself, seemingly separate from their choice. This view makes sense of the following passages:

- He chose us in him before the foundation of the world, that we should be holy and blameless before him. In love he predestined us for adoption to himself as sons through Jesus Christ, according to the purpose of his will.... (Ephesians 1:4-5)

- So too at the present time there is a remnant, chosen by grace. But if it is by grace, it is no longer on the basis of works; otherwise grace would no longer be grace. (Romans 11:5-6)
- For we know, brothers loved by God, that he has chosen you, because our gospel came to you not only in word, but also in power and in the Holy Spirit and with full conviction. You know what kind of men we proved to be among you for your sake. (1 Thessalonians 1:4-5)
- For God has not destined us for wrath, but to obtain salvation through our Lord Jesus Christ. (1 Thessalonians 5:9)
- [God] saved us and called us to a holy calling, not because of our works but because of his own purpose and grace, which he gave us in Christ Jesus before the ages began. (2 Timothy 1:9)

This complicates things! If God can predestine individuals, and His highest desire is for all to be saved, then why doesn't He just predestine *everyone* to be saved? And how does human freedom play into all this? Their answers seem to lie outside the realm of human understanding. In theological terms, they are inscrutable. This is likely, but should we be content with such resignation? A sixteenth-century Spanish priest wasn't. His name was Luis de Molina, and he devised a theory of providence that boldly declares to answer these paradoxes. The next section will examine his theory and see if it truly resolves them.

2

Molinism Described

M olinism attempts to reconcile the paradoxes we described in the previous chapter. This theological model derives its name from Luis de Molina, a 16th century Jesuit counter-reformer. Molina saw the center of the Reformation as a wholesale rejection of human freedom and a collapse into causal determinism.[8] He strove to offer Luther and the Reformers an alternative model that affirmed both human freedom and God's sovereignty. This is Molinism summarized: God uses His knowledge of counterfactuals (middle knowledge), contingent upon human freedom, to providentially arrange a world that brings about the maximum amount of saved individuals. We'll spend the rest of the chapter discussing this definition.

Molinism begins by identifying three kinds of divine knowledge. The first is God's natural knowledge of everything that *could* happen or *could* be. The second is God's middle knowledge of everything that *would* happen under various circumstances. The third is God's free knowledge of everything that *will* happen in the Actual World, our current reality.[9]

God's natural and free knowledge are uncontroversial, but

Molinism says that He also has *middle knowledge* of everything that *would* happen in various circumstances. Middle knowledge concerns statements known as counterfactual conditionals, or simply counterfactuals. They are characterized by "if...would." Some examples are: If I were rich, I would buy a private island. If Hillary had been elected, Obama would have thrown a party. If you ask her out, she would say yes. We get the term *counterfactual* because the statements are typically contrary to what is factual. But the term is broader than that. We can talk about *true* counterfactuals and *false* counterfactuals. A true counterfactual is that Peter, if found in those precise circumstances at the crucifixion, *would deny* Christ. A false counterfactual is that Peter, if found in those precise circumstances at the crucifixion, *would affirm* Christ. The important thing to remember about counterfactuals (whether true or false) is simply the construction "if...would."

The evidence for God's knowledge of counterfactuals is twofold. First, counterfactuals are natural to the way we think and speak. We know the difference between what someone *could* do and what someone *would* do. An introvert *could* spontaneously, with no provocation, scream and howl in a crowded restaurant. That is within the realm of possibility. But he or she probably *would* not do such a thing. As humans, we only have probable knowledge of counterfactuals. I can say, "He or she *probably* would not do such a thing," but only God can say, "He or she *certainly* would not."

Second, Scripture is full of counterfactual language, often attributed to God. A famous prooftext for Molinism is Jesus' condemnation of Chorazin and Bethsaida, which was discussed in Section One. We will consider it again.

> Then he began to denounce the cities where most of his mighty works had been done, because they did not repent. "Woe to you, Chorazin! Woe to you, Bethsaida! For if the

mighty works done in you had been done in Tyre and Sidon, they would have repented long ago in sackcloth and ashes. But I tell you, it will be more bearable on the day of judgment for Tyre and Sidon than for you. And you, Capernaum, will you be exalted to heaven? You will be brought down to Hades. For if the mighty works done in you had been done in Sodom, it would have remained until this day. But I tell you that it will be more tolerable on the day of judgment for the land of Sodom than for you." (Matthew 11:20-24)

Here, Jesus reveals His counterfactual knowledge of what the people in Tyre and Sidon *would* have done if He had performed miracles there. Another famous proof text of God's knowledge of counterfactuals is 1 Samuel 23:8-14.

And Saul summoned all the people to war, to go down to Keilah, to besiege David and his men. David knew that Saul was plotting harm against him. And he said to Abiathar the priest, "Bring the ephod here." Then David said, "O Lord, the God of Israel, your servant has surely heard that Saul seeks to come to Keilah, to destroy the city on my account. Will the men of Keilah surrender me into his hand? Will Saul come down, as your servant has heard? O Lord, the God of Israel, please tell your servant." And the Lord said, "He will come down." Then David said, "Will the men of Keilah surrender me and my men into the hand of Saul?" And the Lord said, "They will surrender you." Then David and his men, who were about six hundred, arose and departed from Keilah, and they went wherever they could go. When Saul was told that David had escaped from Keilah, he gave up the expedition. And David remained in the strongholds in the wilderness, in the hill country of the wilderness of Ziph. And Saul sought him every day, but God did not give him into his hand.

Here, God reveals His counterfactual knowledge of what Saul and the men of Keilah *would* do if David stayed in his current location. On this passage, Molina writes, "Notice, God knew these two future contingents, which depended on human choice, and He revealed them to David. Yet they never have existed and never will exist in reality, and thus they do not exist in eternity either."[10] Other passages support the notion of divine middle knowledge. They require little exposition.

- "For you are not sent to a people of foreign speech and a hard language, but to the house of Israel— not to many peoples of foreign speech and a hard language, whose words you cannot understand. Surely, if I sent you to such, they would listen to you." (Ezekiel 3:5-6)
- Then Jeremiah said to Zedekiah, "Thus says the Lord, the God of hosts, the God of Israel: If you will surrender to the officials of the king of Babylon, then your life shall be spared, and this city shall not be burned with fire, and you and your house shall live. But if you do not surrender to the officials of the king of Babylon, then this city shall be given into the hand of the Chaldeans, and they shall burn it with fire, and you shall not escape from their hand." (Jeremiah 38:17-18)
- "None of the rulers of this age understood this, for if they had, they would not have crucified the Lord of glory." (1 Corinthians 2:8)
- "And if you had known what this means, 'I desire mercy, and not sacrifice,' you would not have condemned the guiltless." (Matthew 12:7)

- "And he said, 'No, father Abraham, but if someone goes to them from the dead, they will repent.' He said to him, 'If they do not hear Moses and the Prophets, neither will they be convinced if someone should rise from the dead." (Luke 16:30-31)
- "If you are the Christ, tell us." But he said to them, "If I tell you, you will not believe, and if I ask you, you will not answer." (Luke 22:67-68)
- "If I had not come and spoken to them, they would not have been guilty of sin, but now they have no excuse for their sin. Whoever hates me hates my Father also. If I had not done among them the works that no one else did, they would not be guilty of sin, but now they have seen and hated both me and my Father." (John 15:22-24)
- Jesus answered, "My kingdom is not of this world. If my kingdom were of this world, my servants would have been fighting, that I might not be delivered over to the Jews. But my kingdom is not from the world." (John 18:36)

After making the case for middle knowledge, we must also note the differences between Possible, Feasible, and Actual Worlds. Each of them pair with natural, middle, and free knowledge, respectively. First a word about what philosophers mean by *world*. In the philosophical sense, a World isn't a planet, per se, or any concrete object—or even a universe. It's simply a complete description of a possible reality. In another World, the constellations might be different. In another World, Pluto might not exist. In another World, the continents might be arranged differently. These are Possible Worlds. The Actual World is the description that is true. A Feasible World is any Possible World that is feasible for God to actualize (bring into existence) given the circumstances of human freedom. Some

Christians might feel uncomfortable with the notion that God could not actualize any Possible World He wishes, but this goes back to the argument in Section One on the logical impossibility of God creating causally-determined free agents. So, we have a range of Possible Worlds with a subset of Feasible Worlds, and one of those Feasible Worlds is the Actual World.[11]

Molinist Model
Logical Order of Events

Possible Worlds	**Worlds**
Contains all true and false counterfactuals	OOOOO
Feasible Worlds	**Worlds**
Contains all and only true counterfactuals	O OO
God's Divine Decree	
Actual World	**Worlds**
Contains all and only true counterfactuals of the World God chose to actualize	O

Molinism says that God surveyed these worlds in three moments. He surveyed the range of Possible Worlds, determined which ones were Feasible, and then—by Divine Decree—chose one of them to be the Actual World. These moments are not chronological, but rather logical. They do not occur in time, but rather in logical succession.

> To say that something is logically prior to something else is *not* to say that the one occurs before the other in time. Temporally, they could be simultaneous. Rather, logical priority means that something serves to explain something else. The one provides the grounds or basis for the other.[12]

Likewise, Molinism proposes three logical moments in God's knowledge. In the first moment, using His natural knowledge, God surveyed the range of Possible Worlds. In the second moment, using His middle knowledge, God determined which ones were Feasible. Given sin's universality, it is impossible for God to actualize the World in which everyone is saved (Section Three, Soteriology). Then, by Divine Decree, He chose one of those to be the Actual World. In the third moment, using His free knowledge, God knows all that will happen in the world He has created.[13]

Let's set up a hypothetical situation to illustrate how Molinism works. Ashley and Manuel are classmates at a university. One day, Manuel decides to ask out Ashley. However, her answer depends upon whether a storm passes through the city the previous night or not. So we have a natural event (a stormy night or a clear night) and a human-freedom event (Ashley saying yes or no). This situation gives us a number of Possible Worlds. We will examine six. (These are not all the Possible Worlds regarding this situation, but we need to limit our investigation for the sake of illustration.)

Possible Worlds
1. The night is clear, and Ashley says yes.
2. The night is clear, and Ashley says no.
3. The night is clear, and Ashley walks away without answering.
4. The night is stormy, and Ashley says yes.
5. The night is stormy, and Ashley says no.
6. The night is stormy, and Ashley walks away without answering.

Whether a storm passes through or not, Ashley *could* say yes, no, or refuse to answer. Those are six Possible Worlds. However, given Ashley's temperament, personality, inherited genetic tendencies, parental involvement throughout childhood, and a host of other factors, we know that Ashley is decisive and *would not* walk away without answering, regardless of whether a storm passes or not. If another girl were in her situation, she may act differently. But we're dealing with Ashley. Possible Worlds 3 and 6 are infeasible.

We must consider not only Ashley's personality, but also the storm. Ashley is easily irritable. A stormy night would disrupt her sleep, put her in a bad mood, and she *would* say no. However, if the night is clear, then Ashley would get a good night's rest and she *would* say yes. Those are two true counterfactuals: If the night is stormy, then she would say no. If the night is clear, then she would say yes. Possible Worlds 2 and 4 are infeasible. Among the six Possible Worlds, the only Feasible Worlds are 1 and 5.

Feasible Worlds
1. The night is clear, and Ashley says yes.
5. The night is stormy, and Ashley says no.

God chooses one of these worlds to actualize. Let's hypothesize that He actualizes the Feasible World in which the night is stormy and Ashley says no. The reason is because He has ordained that she marry another. Poor Manuel.

Actual World
5. The night is stormy, and Ashley says no.

And that's how Molinism works.

But let's further hypothesize that God, by way of the storm, uses Ashley's refusal of Manuel to direct her to another man, and that relationship culminates in her conversion to Christianity. That is why God actualizes Feasible World 5. If so, then Ashley's choice to say no to Manuel aids in bringing about her later conversion. This shows that none of our decisions are neutral. Even seemingly inconsequential decisions have major repercussions regarding salvation.

This leads into an essential notion: All events are causally linked. For some reason, some theologians assume that God can choose some events in the world, but leave others to human freedom. And that is how they reconcile providence and human freedom. Personally, I have heard this formulated to say that God chooses people to be saved, but we are free to choose everything else. I may freely drive to either Subway or Chili's for lunch, but I cannot freely choose to accept or reject God's offer of salvation.

However, this position is logically untenable. It logically concludes in *causal determinism*. That is, God determines every decision, action, and event.[14] This is because it is impossible to draw a line between choice and non-choice within the same universe. Let's say I freely choose to go to Subway for lunch. There, I have a conversation with someone and it leads to him being saved. That would make God's predestination of that individual entirely dependent upon my free choice to drive to Subway. It would make mankind sovereign over salvation. It would do no good to say that God determines my driving to Subway but nothing else, because I would first need to freely buy a car, freely fill its tank with gas, freely apply and get a job to pay for the sandwich, and so on. The only logically sustainable position for proponents of this view is causal determinism. God determines every word, thought, step, glance, decision, action, natural event, etc. So if we don't have a choice in salvation, then we don't have a choice in anything.

Numerous problems trouble causal determinism. Christian philosopher William Lane Craig lists five: 1) Universal, divine, causal determinism cannot offer a coherent interpretation of Scripture, 2) Universal causal determinism cannot be rationally affirmed, 3) Universal, divine, determinism makes God the author of sin and precludes human responsibility, 4) Universal, divine, determinism nullifies human agency, and 5) Universal, divine determinism makes reality into a farce.[15]

Luis de Molina dealt with a similar objection. His critics claimed that God directs all moral acts, but leaves immoral acts to human freedom. In *Concordia IV: On Divine Foreknowledge*, he says this to them:

> Many things depended on the sins of Adam's descendants. For instance, the death of Christ, the redemption of the human race, and all the things that followed therefrom depended on the sins of the Jews; the crowns of the martyrs depended on the sins of tyrants; acts of adultery, sacrilege, and incest, as well as other acts of fornication, led to the procreation of all those who were generated by such acts of fornication, and thus led to the doing of all those things, both good and evil, that were going to be done by the free choice of those so procreated....Thus it follows that many of the *good* things that were going to occur because of the human faculty of choice from the beginning of the world up to its consummation would not have been known with certainty by God as absolutely future except because of middle knowledge, a knowledge through which He knew that the *sins* on which those things depended were going to occur, on the hypothesis that the order of things which was in fact produced at the beginning should be produced by Him.[16]

Great quote. Molina concludes that God must direct, as some level, all the actions of humans, and yet humans also must do them of their own freedom. God's ordination and human freedom must work together in all events of the world. All events are causally linked, and so it is impossible to say, "God determines some individuals to do certain things, but leaves other things to their own freedom." All actions, evil and good together, are both directed by God and yet also done from human freedom. God's middle knowledge seems to be the only way to reconcile this apparent paradox.

Another reason God must direct events using middle knowledge pertains to what Molina calls the *freedom of contradiction*. Mankind cannot be guilty of rejecting God unless they had genuine freedom to do differently. Likewise, they cannot be rewarded for *accepting* God unless they had genuine freedom to do differently. And yet God must somehow direct the future with certainty, simultaneously allowing for human freedom. The only way this can occur is through God's middle knowledge of counterfactuals. Molina writes,

> Just as, in order for an act to be a *sin* it is not sufficient that it be spontaneous, but is instead necessary that it be free in such a way that, when the faculty of choice consents to it, it has the power not to consent to it, given all the surrounding circumstances obtaining at the time, so too in order for there to be *merit* or for an act to be *morally* good—indeed, even in order for there to be a free act that is indifferent to moral good and evil—it is necessary that when the act is elicited by the faculty of choice, it be within the faculty's power not to elicit it, given all the circumstances obtaining at that time. This, of course, is the freedom which is called the *freedom of contradiction*, and which is the very least that has to be present for an act to be called free, even if the act is only indifferent with regard to moral good and evil.[17]

God somehow directs all events, and yet humans perform evil acts. If humans did not have the freedom of contradiction (the freedom to act contrary to God's plan), then they could not be guilty of personal sin. If we are not guilty of sin, then Christ's death and resurrection is meaningless. And yet, even though we *could* act contrary to God's plan, we simply *would not* because God has perfect knowledge of what we *would* do and directs things accordingly. Middle knowledge is the only way God could both direct the events of the world, and yet not be responsible for the evil that occurs in it.

One more thing must be discussed before ending this section. One version of Molinism says that all the individuals who are lost in the Actual World would be lost in all other Possible and Feasible Worlds. That is, the individuals who freely reject God in this world would freely reject Him in all circumstances. There are no circumstances in which they would freely accept God. This doctrine is called *transworld damnation*. The damned in this world would be damned in all worlds. I find this idea unacceptable for three reasons. First, claiming that the majority of humanity could not be saved in any given circumstance seems to unnecessarily limit God's omnipotence. It is one thing to claim that God cannot perform logical impossibilities, it is another to claim that most individuals are logically impossible to save. Second, it would seem to make irrelevant the grace given to humanity through the Moral Law, saying that it is ineffective in most of the humans God creates (discussed in Section Three, Soteriology). Third, this seems to contradict many of the classic Molinist proof texts, such as Matthew 11:20-24. Here, Jesus clearly states that the individuals of Tyre and Sidon rejected God, but they *would* have accepted Him had the circumstances been different (i.e. had God actualized a different Feasible World). It seems odd to be a Molinist and yet dismiss the clear Molinist implications of this proof text. I conclude that each individual could be saved in some given circumstance. Yet God actualizes the Feasible World in which the maximum amount freely accept Him.

God is omnipotent, omniscient, and omnibenevolent and desires all peoples to be saved, yet many are eternally separated from Him. He sovereignly elects individuals to salvation, yet individuals choose God. He directs all events, yet humans freely make choices. These paradoxes can be explained using

God's middle knowledge. Molinism's two main pillars are 1) God's providence via middle knowledge, and 2) the human freedom of contradiction. So far, I have yet to encounter a theory of divine providence that can explain all of these paradoxes with such simplicity.

William Hasker is an open theist and vigorous opponent of Molinism, but he says this,

> If you are committed to a 'strong' view of providence, according to which, down to the smallest detail, 'things are as they are because God knowingly decided to create such a world,' and yet you also wish to maintain a libertarian conception of free will—if this is what you want, then Molinism is the only game in town.[18]

3

Molinism Applied

G od's middle knowledge has enormous explanatory power. I view it as a theological Swiss-army knife. It has been applied to the issues of Christian particularism,[19] perseverance of the saints,[20] biblical inspiration,[21] biblical infallibility,[22] Christology,[23] the fall and natural evil,[24] quantum indeterminism,[25] and others. This section will examine six theological areas of discussion.

Soteriology

In many ways, this book has already presented a Molinist view of soteriology. However, it must be explicitly stated. Given the logical impossibility of suspending human freedom, God surveyed all Possible Worlds, determined which ones were feasible, and then actualized one. Given His genuine love for all persons in the whole world (John 3:16), God likely actualized a Feasible World that brings about the maximum amount of individuals who freely respond to His global offer of salvation. God chooses which world to actualize and in that way predestines individuals of that world unto salvation. Yet individuals still freely choose Him according to His divine direction. God chooses individuals (predestines them) and uses His middle knowledge to direct them to freely choose Him. One French Molinist says it this way: "It is up to God whether I find myself in a world in which I am predestined; But it is up to me whether I am predestined in the world in which I find myself." In this way, discussions are settled of whether God is wholly responsible for choosing individuals or individuals are wholly responsible for choosing God: They are both responsible for choosing each other.

But there is more to it, of course. Some Christians persuasively argue that mankind cannot choose God, that mankind is "totally depraved" and has no ability to seek after God. After all, Romans 3:10 says, "There is none righteous, no, not one." And other verses clearly state that mankind is spiritually dead (Colossians 2:13). In the same way that a corpse cannot respond to physical stimuli, so mankind cannot respond to spiritual stimuli. He must be revived wholly as an act of God apart from any human act or response. When people choose God, it is because God moved and stirred their faculty to choose Him. They could do no else.

The objection is persuasive to many, so let's begin by looking at the relation between sin and mankind. The first point is that sin is universal. It permeates everything. Romans 5:12 says, "Therefore, just as sin came into the world through one man, and death through sin, and so death spread to all men because all sinned." All individuals are tainted by sin because of Adam's transgression. Romans 5:18 says, "one trespass led to condemnation for all men." Not only does sin permeate everything and everyone, it also condemns everyone, rendering each individual guilty. Romans 3:23 says, "For all have sinned and fall short of the glory of God." Sin is universal and permeates all mankind, separating them from God. It does not mean that mankind is wholly sinful, or that mankind has no conscience. It simply means that sin permeates everything. Some theologians have used the analogy of a drop of ink in a glass of water. The glass does not turn wholly to ink, but the ink has wholly permeated the water. Sin is like the drop of ink, wholly permeating but not wholly transforming.

The second point is that Scripture uses the language of "death" to describe mankind's spiritual state. Here are some examples.

- Therefore, just as sin came into the world through one man, and death through sin, and so death spread to all men because all sinned. (Romans 5:12)
- In Adam all die.... (1 Corinthians 5:22)
- And you, who were dead in your trespasses and the uncircumcision of your flesh, God made alive together with him, having forgiven us all our trespasses.... (Colossians 2:13)
- You were dead in the trespasses and sins in which you once walked.... (Ephesians 2:1-2)

It can be tempting to interpret these too literally, that is, interpret them to mean that mankind has no ability to respond to spiritual stimuli and that, to be saved, mankind must be divinely revived wholly as an act of God. Plenty of passages can be pointed out to discourage such a literal interpretation. We will begin with the Parable of the Prodigal Son. Here, a father has two sons. One of them takes an early inheritance, travels to a far country, and squanders everything in reckless living. He comes to his senses and returns home, repentant. The father responds in a beautiful way,

But the father said to his servants, 'Bring quickly the best robe, and put it on him, and put a ring on his hand, and shoes on his feet. And bring the fattened calf and kill it, and let us eat and celebrate. For this my son was dead, and is alive again; he was lost, and is found.' And they began to celebrate. (Luke 15:22-24)

In the same way that the prodigal son was separated from his father's love and was "dead," so we humans are separated from God's love and are "dead." But this does not mean we cannot respond to spiritual stimuli, or that we cannot seek God, or that we do not have a conscience, or any of those things. Rather, being "dead in our sins" simply means that we are deeply separated from God's love and must be restored in relationship to Him. We are "dead," but when we accept God's love, then we are made "alive."

We have two other reasons to discourage a literal interpretation of mankind's dead spiritual state. First is the arguments made in favor of human freedom made in Section One. Second is the Moral Law written on our hearts which serves as the means by which mankind can sense God and seek after Him, even though we are permeated by sin and dead to God's love. Romans 2 speaks of the Moral Law.

He will render to each one according to his works: to those who by patience in well-doing seek for glory and honor and immortality, he will give eternal life; but for those who are self-seeking and do not obey the truth, but obey unrighteousness, there will be wrath and fury. There will be tribulation and distress for every human being who does evil, the Jew first and also the Greek, but glory and honor and peace for everyone who does good, the Jew first and also the Greek. For God shows no partiality. (Romans 2:6-11)

For when Gentiles, who do not have the law, by nature do what the law requires, they are a law to themselves, even though they do not have the law. They show that the work of the law is written on their hearts, while their conscience also bears witness, and their conflicting thoughts accuse or even excuse them on that day when, according to my gospel, God judges the secrets of men by Christ Jesus. (Romans 2:14-16)

The Moral Law is clearly given by God as an intrinsic means by which humans may sense God and seek Him. This further discourages the view that humans are spiritually dead in the literal sense.

However, Romans 3:10-12 is another passage often used to defend a literal interpretation of mankind's dead spiritual state.

As it is written:
"There is none righteous, no, not one;
There is none who understands;
There is none who seeks after God.
They have all turned aside;
They have together become unprofitable;
There is none who does good, no, not one."

On its face, this passage seems to clearly state that no individual on the face of the planet seeks after God. However, let's turn to Genesis 6:5, which states, "The LORD saw that the wickedness of man was great in the earth, and that every intention of the thoughts of his heart was only evil continually." Of course, this excludes Noah who "found grace in the eyes of the LORD" (v. 8). Clearly, Genesis 6:5 is hyperbole. Even though "every intention of his heart was only evil continually," Noah is an exception. Romans 3:10-12 may be hyperbole in the same way. In general, mankind does not seek after God. (*Does not* is different than *cannot*.) The exception is those who are predestined to come to a saving knowledge of Him.

But we do have passages of grace to understand. Ephesians 2:8-9 says, "For by grace you have been saved through faith.

And this is not your own doing; it is the gift of God, not a result of works, so that no one may boast." William Lane Craig discusses this particular passage.

> Doesn't this [Ephesians 2:8-9] show that faith is simply God's gift to you and not something that you do on your own? I think that is incorrect and I think demonstrably so. Let me ask those of you who are our vigilant Logos software users to tell us what is the gender of the word for "faith" that is used in verse 8? I should mention here that in Greek, as in modern day German, every noun has a gender. There are three genders—masculine, feminine, and neuter. It is the same in Greek. Now, what is the gender of the word *pistis* or *faith?* Feminine. So it is feminine gender for *pistis* or *faith.* What is the gender of the pronoun in verse 8 "this." Neuter! *Touto* is the word. It is neuter. So the antecedent of "this" is not the word "faith." You would have to have a feminine pronoun in order to refer to "faith." Rather, what the word "this" refers to is the whole preceding clause, namely, salvation by grace through faith. That is not your own doing. This is the gift of God. This is the way God has elected to set it up; he is going to save by his grace everyone who has faith in Christ. That is not your own doing. But it does not teach that saving faith is the gift of God. That is grammatically prohibited.[27]

To emphasize: "*[God] is going to save by his grace everyone who has faith in Christ.*" God is not required to save mankind. He could simply walk away (figuratively) and leave us in sin and death, separated from Himself. But He doesn't. By grace, God directs the events of the world to draw us toward Himself. Intrinsically, He writes the Moral Law on our hearts that we might have the ability to sense Him and seek Him. Extrinsically, He uses methods such as tragedy and loss, or the beauty and order of creation, or the loving evangelism of a friend to direct individuals to freely repent of their sin and accept His global offer of salvation. In theological terms, the Moral Law functions as both prevenient grace and common grace.

In Molinist fashion, we might understand God's grace in soteriology this way.

Possible Worlds
(More worlds exist than just these three)
1. All mankind accepts God.
2. Accounting for human freedom, the maximum amount of individuals accept God.
3. All mankind rejects God.

Feasible Worlds
(World 1 is infeasible because of sin's universality)
2. Accounting for human freedom, the maximum amount of individuals accept God.
3. All mankind rejects God.

Actual World
2. Accounting for freedom, the maximum amount of individuals accept God.

God actualizes a world in which the maximum amount of individuals freely accept His global offer of salvation. He wasn't required to do so, but out of His great love for humanity He sent His son into the torment of the crucifixion so that He might defeat death and provide a way of salvation. Then God used extrinsic means of world events and circumstances to operate upon the Moral Law written on our hearts to bring us into a state of repentance where we freely accept His love and salvation.[28]

Problem of Evil

The ancient Greek philosopher Epicurus (ca. 341-270 BC) is generally credited with first arguing that the existence of evil refutes the existence of God. His argument reemerges nearly every generation in different forms, but has largely remained the same. He formulated it this way:

Is God willing to prevent evil, but not able? Then he is not omnipotent.
Is he able, but not willing? Then he is malevolent.
Is he both able and willing? Then whence cometh evil?
Is he neither able nor willing? Then why call him God?

After hundreds of years, Epicurus' objection still challenges theists: Either God can't stop evil, or He won't stop evil. Many good responses can be made to say that God has some higher plan and that we are cognitively limited in knowing how evil contributes to it. (Genesis 50:20 is a good example.) And those are fine answers, but they are not particularly Molinist.

Molinism states that God's highest desire is the salvation of all peoples, and the reason He does not achieve this desire is because of human freedom (Section One). Essentially, Molinism bites the Epicurean bullet, so to speak, and states that God *can't* stop evil. Stopping evil requires that God suspend human freedom, but that is a logically impossible thing to do. And logical impossibilities are contrary to His nature. They lie outside the proper definition of omnipotence as having *maximal power* (Section One). Molinist theologian Kirk R. MacGregor writes, "While God's absolute will is for each individual to find salvation freely, for no individual to sin freely, and for no natural evil to occur, it is logically impossible for God to create a world where this scenario would transpire."[29]

Some try to say that God's highest desire is His own glory,

and allowing evil and damning most of humanity somehow achieves this goal (Section One). But this just bites the Epicurean bullet a different way: God *won't* stop evil. This seems to make God selfish and deny His omnibenevolence. How does the damnation of most of humanity glorify God? If someone responds to this with, "He desires His own glory for the purpose of drawing humanity to Himself," then why isn't everyone saved? Either God desires all peoples to be saved and human freedom hinders this desire, or God allows evil purely for the sake of glorifying Himself and the salvation of a few humans is merely a means to this end. And so Molinism says that God *can't* stop evil.

This makes sense of spiritual warfare. 1 John 5:19 says, "The whole world lies in the power of the evil one." Jesus called Satan the "ruler of this world" (John 12:31; 14:30; 16:11). Satan is depicted as possessing "all the kingdoms of the world" to the point where he distributes authority as he pleases (Luke 4:5-6). Paul calls Satan the "god of this world" (2 Corinthians 4:4) and the "prince of the power of the air" (Ephesians 2:2). Jesus' earthly ministry was understood to be driving back Satan's kingdom to make way for God's kingdom. Peter says that He "went about doing good and healing all who were oppressed by the devil" (Acts 10:38). Paul eloquently says, "For we do not wrestle against flesh and blood, but against the rulers, against the authorities, against the cosmic powers over this present darkness, against the spiritual forces of evil in the heavenly places" (Ephesians 6:12). If God had complete control over evil, then these passages seem like mere literary decorations, rather than a description of spiritual reality.[30] A war is raging and all free agents are involved, whether we like it or not.

Biblical Inspiration

Methods of how to approach the Bible vary considerably. This is because theologians are met with considerable tensions that are not easily resolved, one of which concerns biblical inspiration. One the one hand, Jesus and the apostles clearly treated the Old and New Testaments as God's Word, the content of which was somehow directed by God. But on the other hand, these same writings contain clear human elements.

Jesus clearly treated the Old Testament as inspired by God. He frequently references events and people that are presumably historical, such as Abel (Luke 11:51), Noah (Matthew 24:37-39), Abraham (John 8:56), Sodom and Gomorrah (Matthew 10:15, 11:23-24; Luke 10:12), Lot (Luke 17:28-32), Isaac and Jacob (Matthew 8:11; Luke 13:28), David eating the shewbread (Matthew 12:3-4; Mark 2:25-26; Luke 6:3-4), Solomon (Matthew 6:29, 12:42; Luke 11:31, 12:27), Elijah (Luke 4:25-26), and many others.[31] He frequently refers to the Old Testament as the "Scriptures" (Luke 4:21; Matthew 21:42; Mark 12:10; Luke 20:17; Psalm 118:22; Matthew 26:54; John 5:39, 7:38). In the account of His temptation, he prefaces each of His quotations of the Old Testament with "It is written" (Matthew 4; Luke 4). The Old Testament obviously carries the authority of God to be used against Satan in such a manner. As John Wenham writes,

> To Christ the Old Testament was true, authoritative, inspired. To him the God of the Old Testament was the living God and the teaching of the Old Testament was the teaching of the living God. To him what Scripture said, God said.[32]

Jesus also clearly treated the New Testament, which was written by the apostles, as being inspired by God. He entrusted

His apostles with carrying on His mission and teaching the gospel in His absence. He says to Peter,

> "And I tell you, you are Peter, and on this rock I will build my church, and the gates of hell shall not prevail against it. I will give you the keys of the kingdom of heaven, and whatever you bind on earth shall be bound in heaven, and whatever you loose on earth shall be loosed in heaven." (Matthew 16:18-19)

He even entrusted the disciples with forgiving and retaining sins (John 20:23). He also likens the Father sending Him to His sending of the apostles. This elevates their authority above mere human teachers (John 20:21). And finally, the Holy Spirit was sent to guide their teaching.

> "When the Spirit of truth comes, he will guide you into all the truth, for he will not speak on his own authority, but whatever he hears he will speak, and he will declare to you the things that are to come." (John 16:13)

It hardly needs to be argued that if Jesus considered the Old Testament to be inspired by God, then so did the apostles. But what did they think about their own writings, that is, the New Testament? Peter claims to be an apostle through which the Lord commands (2 Peter 3:2). He also calls Paul's letters "Scriptures" (2 Peter 3:15-16). Paul claims to be the recipient of special revelation (Ephesians 3:3-5), the Lord entrusted him with preaching (Titus 1:3), and he claims to have received the Gospel from Christ, not man (Galatians 1:12). He claims his message is God's Gospel (2 Corinthians 11:7). Paul also claims, "And we impart this in words not taught by human wisdom but taught by the Spirit, interpreting spiritual truths to those who are spiritual" (1 Corinthians 2:13). With these affirmations from Jesus and the apostles, Paul writes, "All Scripture is breathed out by God and profitable for teaching, for reproof, for correction, and for training in righteousness" (2 Timothy 3:16).

However, in spite of the content of Scripture being clearly directed by God—indeed, its very words—we still observe distinctly human elements that redirect us from a wooden dictation theory of inspiration. These include different authorial styles, cognitive limitations such as Paul displaying memory lapses while writing Scripture (1 Corinthians 1:14-16), uninspired authors interjecting into Scripture (Romans 16:22), and so on. How can the Bible be God's Word, directed and inspired by Him, yet contain clearly human elements?

Via middle knowledge! Molinism says that God directed, from before the foundation of the world, that Scripture would be written using human freedom. For example, if God wanted to direct the writing of the book of Romans, He would create a Paul of Tarsus exactly how He wanted, place him in first-century Palestine, and then Paul *would* freely write the book of Romans. Paul would communicate what God wanted to communicate, but also use his own personality, cultural viewpoints, family background, and cognitive limitations. In this way, God directs the writing of Scripture, yet it is also the product of human freedom.

Princeton theologian B. B. Warfield hit upon a concept of biblical inspiration remarkably similar to Molinism.

For, of course, these books [of the Bible] were not produced suddenly, by some miraculous act handed down complete out of heaven, as the phrase goes; but, like all other products of time, are the ultimate effect of many processes cooperating through long periods.... And there is the preparation of the men to write these books to be considered, a preparation physical, intellectual, spiritual, which must have attended them throughout their whole lives, and, indeed, must have had its beginning in their remote ancestors, and the effect of which was to bring the right men to the right places at the right times, with the right endowments, impulses, acquirements, to write just the books which were designed for them…. Representations are sometimes made as if, when God wished to produce sacred books which would incorporate His will a series of letters like those of Paul, for example, He was reduced to the necessity of going down to earth and painfully scrutinizing the men He found there, seeking anxiously for the one who, on the whole, promised best for His purpose; and then violently forcing the material He wished expressed through him, against his natural bent, and with as little loss from his recalcitrant characteristics as possible. Of course, nothing of the sort took place. If God wished to give His people a series of letters like Paul's He prepared a Paul to write them, and the Paul He brought to the task was a Paul who spontaneously *would write* just such letters.[33] (emphasis mine)

Theologians have struggled for centuries with how to reconcile the apparent paradox of biblical inspiration with human intervention and authorship. But Molinism provides a simple answer: via God's middle knowledge. The answer is effective enough to encourage more investigation into how the Bible reached its present state, without succumbing to a wooden dictation theory. Yet it still attributes the result to God and retains a belief in the Bible's divine authority.

Perseverance of the Saints

Once someone accepts Christ as Lord and Savior, can they fall away? Some theologians answer with a firm *yes* while others answer with a firm *no*. Both find strong passages to support their position, and the Scriptures seem to send mixed messages. Passages used to support eternal security include Ephesians 1:13-14; Philippians 1:6; Romans 8:28-39; John 10:27-30, 6:37-47, 5:24; and Ephesians 4:30-32. Passages used to support conditional security include Romans 11:17-24; Galatians 5:4; Colossians 1:23; 1 Thessalonians 3:5; 1 Timothy 1:19-20; 2 Timothy 2:17-18; James 5:19-20; 2 Peter 2:20-22; 1 John 5:16; and Hebrews 6:1-8, 10:26-31, 4:11.

Molinism itself does not take a stand regarding the perseverance of the saints. Someone may answer the question either *yes* or *no* and still be a Molinist. However, one possible Molinist understanding is this: Yes, believers *can* fall away, but they *won't*. The Scriptural warnings themselves serve as the means by which to keep believers in a relationship with Christ. So, believers *could* fall away (in some Possible World), but they simply *won't*. God has arranged the circumstances to preserve their relationship with Him. Jesus seems to imply this conclusion in John 16:1, "I have said all these things to you to keep you from falling away."

William Lane Craig takes this position. He also makes the observation that if believers *cannot* fall away from the faith, then the warnings against it are superfluous. He elaborates:

> If believers cannot fall away from the faith, then the warnings seem superfluous. However, if it's true that if the warnings had not been given then God would have provided some *other* means of guaranteeing that the believer would persevere in grace, then that view seems indistinguishable from the Molinist view. What lies at the heart of the issue is the efficacy of God's grace: Is God's grace intrinsically efficacious, or is it extrinsically efficacious? If intrinsically, then why the warnings? If extrinsically, then the warnings is the means by which God preserves His elect.[34]

Prayer

Scripture offers plenty of reasons to think that prayer changes the course of world events and so affects who is saved and who isn't. Here are a few examples:

> Had it not been for the prayer of Isaac, Rebecca would have remained barren (Genesis 25:21); had it not been for the prayer of Hannah, Samuel never would have been born (1 Samuel 1:10-20); and had it not been for the prayer of Zechariah, John the Baptist would never have been born (Luke 1:13). If at any of these links in the chain making up our world the relevant persons did not pray, the world would be a radically different place than it in fact is.[35]

Many more examples can be pointed out. MacGregor writes, "In these ways, we, through our prayers, are cocreators of the world with God."[36] He says this about a Molinist view of prayers:

> At this point, an even more provocative question arises: does middle knowledge make it possible for God to respond to some of our prayers in such a way that prayers affect the course of the past? ...Now, no prayer can causally impact the past in a contradictory fashion; I cannot successfully pray that something had happened that would preclude a present reality or that a past event had never occurred.... In other words, I cannot pray to *change* the past. But barring those things that preclude present realities or past events, I can pray for something to have happened such that God in the past would have brought about precisely that event, and if I did not pray for that event to have happened, God in the past would not have brought about that event. So while the event is chronologically prior to the prayer, my prayer is logically

prior to the event.... Hence even though I cannot *change* the past, through prayer I can *effect* the past.[37]

Ignorance of the past might be a prerequisite to saying a prayer that effects the past. The prayer would be logically prior to the event, even though the prayer is chronologically future. But, as any Christian knows, not every prayer is answered. How might we understand failed prayer in light of Matthew 7:7-11? Here, Jesus is recorded saying,

> Ask, and it will be given to you; seek, and you will find; knock, and it will be opened to you. For everyone who asks receives, and the one who seeks finds, and to the one who knocks it will be opened. Or which one of you, if his son asks him for bread, will give him a stone? Or if he asks for a fish, will give him a serpent? If you then, who are evil, know how to give good gifts to your children, how much more will your Father who is in heaven give good things to those who ask him!

From this passage, we might assume that God answers every prayer. But Molina emphasized the word "good" in relation to prayers. God will give *good* things to those who ask Him. Molina devised four middle-knowledge reasons why a prayer may not fall under the definition of a "good thing."[38]

1. The prayer may be logically impossible (such as praying that $2 + 2 = 5$).
2. The prayer may be logically infeasible (such as praying that a certain individual will accept salvation in circumstances that do not permit it).
3. The prayer may not be ultimately advantageous to the individual.
4. The prayer may not be ultimately advantageous to others.

A Molinist view of prayer believes that it can affect world events, perhaps even effecting the past by being logically prior to the event, even if the prayer is chronologically future. However, given Jesus' qualification of answered prayer being "good things," we can devise some reasons why God does not answer every prayer. As MacGregor writes, "Molina's doctrine of providence thus affords Christians a tremendous level of comfort that they can safely lay bare their emotions before God in prayer, knowing that God will only act on those sentiments that will bring about objective good."[39]

Christian Particularism

In the 11th century, isolated Christian Europe did not struggle much with religious pluralism. But when the Age of Exploration began in the 15th century, Christians began encountering other religions like never before. This led to the question: Is Christianity *really* the only way to God?

Let's look at a few passages. Peter declares to the rulers in Jerusalem, "There is salvation in no one else, for there is no other name under heaven given among men by which we must be saved" (Acts 4:12). Paul argues that just as death came into humanity through one man, so salvation also comes through one man: Jesus Christ (Romans 5:12-21). He also says that there is only "one mediator between God and men, the man Christ Jesus" (1 Timothy 2:5-6). Those who would be saved by this mediator must place their faith in him. Jesus says, "I am the way, and the truth, and the life. No one comes to the Father except through me" (John 14:6). And lest anyone be mistaken, the way to God will be found by few. Jesus also says, "Enter by the narrow gate. For the gate is wide and the way is easy that leads to destruction, and those who enter by it are many. For the gate is narrow and the way is hard that leads to life, and those who find it are few"

(Matthew 7:13-14). The New Testament teaches that Jesus is the only way to God.

So the first difficult question is asked: Do Christians really believe that most of humanity will be eternally separated from God just because they were not fortunate enough to be born in a time and place to hear the Gospel? This seems contrary to God's love and justice.

First, we must remember God's desire to save all peoples (Section One). Second, we must remember that He is unable to do this because of the logical impossibility of creating causally-determined free agents (Section One). And, given the overall tendency of humanity to seek their own sinful desires (Romans 1:21, 1 Corinthians 1:18), therefore it is likely that most of humanity will reject God.

However, this assumes that every individual hears the Gospel. What about those who don't? Paul teaches that every individual, despite not hearing the Gospel, has the Moral Law written on his heart (Romans 2:14-16). It is possible that they respond to this law, and then recognize the existence of a higher power, which is God. If so, then He will grant them eternal life (Romans 2:6-7). But Jesus indicates that few will respond to the Moral Law written on their hearts (Matthew 7:13-14) and stresses the importance of evangelism (Matthew 28:16-20). He lays a heavy burden on Christians to spread the Gospel. It seems that fewer humans will be saved without our evangelistic efforts.

This invites another question: Since God explicitly revealed Himself to Paul and secured his salvation that way (Acts 9:1-19), then why doesn't God explicitly reveal Himself to *every* individual? If human freedom plays no role in salvation, then it is indeed a serious question. But I can think of five possible reasons why God explicitly revealing Himself to each individual on Earth, allowing for human freedom, could be susceptible to drawbacks.

First, it's possible that such brazen openness would cause some individuals to feel pressured into coming to God, and that would make them even more stubborn to His message! Think of romantic human relationships. Most of the time, a subtle and gentle approach is far more effective than being forceful and heavy-handed. Humans tend to resist being pressured into things (we like to make decisions ourselves, thank you very much), resist submitting to authority, and in general be depraved beings. The combination of these traits could cause individuals to react with hostility should God brazenly reveal Himself to them and demand allegiance. Or think of the Pharisees and Sadducees who became even more embittered when they saw Jesus working miracles. Humans are naturally stubborn and don't like to feel pressured into decisions.

Second, it's possible that such revelation would overwhelm some individuals with awe, causing them to submit out of fear, rather than love. Third, it's possible that some individuals may become so enraptured with their divine experience that they neglect their Christian duty to love others and spread His message. An example of this can be seen in Christian monastics who secluded themselves in the desert trying to get closer to God by being alone for years on end. Fourth, it's possible that explicitly revealing Himself to some individuals would cause them to rely on personal experience and reject the life of the mind, stunting spiritual growth.

Finally, it is also possible that it wouldn't make a difference to many individuals. Humans typically shove aside spiritual things in favor of worldly things. They seek power, pleasure, and pride at the expense of the Moral Law. So it is possible that were God to explicitly reveal Himself to some individuals, it would make no difference. They would still reject Him in favor of worldly things. The Parable of the Rich Man and Lazarus illustrates this. The Rich Man is suffering in Hell and Lazarus stands viewing him in Heaven. The Rich Man asks

Abraham to send Lazarus to his brothers so that they will escape Hell's torment. Abraham replies, "If they do not hear Moses and the Prophets, neither will they be convinced if someone should rise from the dead" (Luke 16:31). It's possible some individuals would not repent even if truth were explicitly revealed to them.

One or more of these possible reasons may be why God does not explicitly reveal Himself to individuals. It is logically infeasible for God to ensure the salvation of all peoples since they are free agents who are typically seeking their own desires. As it is, He saves the maximum amount of individuals while allowing for human freedom.

This includes using humans to evangelize to other humans. It's possible God knows via middle knowledge that the vast majority of humanity *would* respond in one of the five ways discussed above, and so decides to use natural means of evangelism rather than supernatural means. For some individuals, perhaps another human would be too threatening, and so God uses the gentler means of natural revelation to direct others toward Himself. They would not receive the full benefit of an explicit relationship with Jesus Christ, which could include heavenly rewards, but nevertheless they are able to come to God through witnessing His attributes within themselves and in creation. How many are saved through general revelation? Perhaps not many, as Jesus indicates (Matthew 7:13-14). And so Christians are given the responsibility of evangelism. In Acts 26:16-18, Jesus explicitly entrusts Paul with the responsibility of opening people's eyes and causing them to place faith in Christ.

> But rise and stand upon your feet, for I have appeared to you
> for this purpose, to appoint you as a servant and witness to
> the things in which you have seen me and to those in which I
> will appear to you, delivering you from your people and from

the Gentiles—to whom I am sending you to open their eyes, so that they may turn from darkness to light and from the power of Satan to God, that they may receive forgiveness of sins and a place among those who are sanctified by faith in me.

But we are not alone in this endeavor. In his message to the Acropolis, Paul indicates that God situates persons so that each have an opportunity to find salvation. He declares,

And [God] made from one man every nation of mankind to live on all the face of the earth, having determined allotted periods and the boundaries of their dwelling place, that they should seek God, and perhaps feel their way toward him and find him. Yet he is actually not far from each one of us.... (Acts 17:26-27)

This is a striking confirmation of a Molinist way of thinking. God arranges circumstances to direct free individuals, by natural means, to Himself. Yet none are left forgotten, for each person has the Moral Law written on his heart through which he may understand the nature of God and seek Him. That is why Pauls says, "For what can be known about God is plain to them, because God has shown it to them. For his invisible attributes, namely, his eternal power and divine nature, have been clearly perceived, ever since the creation of the world, in the things that have been made. So they are without excuse" (Romans 1:19-20). And so, though Earth contains many religions, God arranges circumstances to save the maximum amount of individuals, through natural means and through the actions of evangelists. He does this out of great love for sinners whom He saves by the grace of the crucifixion and the power of the resurrection.

4

Common Objections

L ike any theory of divine providence, Molinism receives its fair share of objections. This section responds to some of the more common ones I've heard. Contemporary scholarly discussions have reached a place where skeptics and proponents recognize two main objections to Molinism: 1) True counterfactuals do not exist, and 2) God cannot have middle knowledge prior to His divine decree.[40] My gut reaction is, "Those objections are so esoteric. If that's the best skeptics can say, then Molinism is doing pretty well for itself." However, I offer brief responses to them, among others. Feel free to skip to whichever objection strikes you. The order is unimportant.

—Molinism shouldn't use philosophy. The unfortunate thing about this objection is that it is far too common. Over the centuries, Christians have used philosophical insights to great theological effect. Even Paul quotes Greek philosophers over a dozen times in support of his theological arguments (Appendix A). If Paul feels comfortable referencing secular philosophers to support a theological point, then Christians should feel comfortable following his lead, provided their conclusions are orthodox and agree with Gospel basics.

But probably the best argument in favor of Christians using philosophy is the orthodox doctrine of the Trinity. In the first few centuries just after Jesus, Christians were struggling to reconcile teachings about God that seemed contradictory. Was there only one God, or three? And how could a man claim to be the Son of God if He was actually God Himself? Greek philosophers immediately accused them of having an incoherent view of God. In response, Christians came up with different theories of God such as Modalism, Arianism, Adoptionism, and so on. But none of these theories accounted for all of the Scriptural data. Each of them interpreted some passages according to their plain meaning, yet ignored others. A different kind of approach was needed.

The early church fathers decided to interpret all of the difficult passages according to their plain meaning and then devise a theological model that makes sense of them. The result was the doctrine of the Trinity. They didn't know it at the time, but they were taking a very scientific approach. They examined all of the Scriptural data before them: passages that support monotheism, passages that distinguish the three divine persons, and passages that use familial language like "Son of God" and "Father." None of the previous theories accounted for them all. After much debate, they settled on two important words: *homoousis* and *hypostases*. God is three persons (*hypostases*), yet one substance (*homoousis*). These are the two pillars of the Christian concept of God. They are Greek words that the Scriptures do not use to describe God, but they sufficiently explain all of the Scriptural data. Because of its explanatory power, the early church fathers adopted the Trinitarian model as orthodox. That is the scientific approach: examine the relevant data, and then devise a model with sufficient explanatory power. (Note: Even though the Trinity is a doctrinal model, it is non-negotiable for orthodox Christians. The early church fathers debated for hundreds of years and concluded that the full divinity of each of the three members of the Godhead, yet still conceived as one God, is absolutely essential for the Gospel.)

Molinism takes a similar approach. Instead of sacrificing the plain meaning of some passages in favor of others, Molinism takes a variety of biblical passages at face value and then devises a theological model with sufficient explanatory power. Like the doctrine of the Trinity, this requires extra-biblical language. I'm not saying that Molinism should be orthodox like the Trinity, but the two models take a similar approach. Sometimes, to understand the Bible, we might need to pull back a bit and look at the wider picture.

—*Molinism is fatalistic.* This objection usually takes the logical form of theological fatalism. It states that if God knows something will happen, then necessarily it will happen. However, this objection fails to recognize one thing: Knowledge is not a causal agent. God's knowledge of an event is not the cause of the event. Similarly, if I know that a plane will depart from Sri Lanka at the break of dawn, my knowledge of that event in no way causes it. If it turns out that the plane is delayed and departs in the afternoon, then I did not have knowledge, I only had belief. That God knows something will happen does not cause the event. So it *could* happen differently. It simply *will not* happen differently. As MacGregor writes, "Knowledge is not causally determinative. That is to say, God's knowledge of what a person would do in some set of circumstances exerts no causal power on the person to act as God knows, just as human knowledge of what other humans would do exerts no causal power over their choices."[41]

Molina and other church fathers (even those who would

not claim to be Molinist), affirm that God's foreknowledge of events do not themselves *cause* the events to happen. Rather, the event causes God's foreknowledge. Several ancient church fathers agree, such as Justin Martyr, Origen, Damascene, Chrysostom, Jerome, Augustine, Cyril, and Leo I.[42] Molina puts it this way,

> For the things that issue forth from our choice or depend on it are not going to happen because they are foreknown by God as going to happen, but, to the contrary, they are foreknown by God as going to happen in this or that way because they are so going to happen by virtue of our freedom of choice.[43]

An objection at this point may be, "But if humankind has the ability to act contrary to what God knows will happen—if they *could* do differently, as you say—then you give humankind the power to frustrate God's plan." That is correct. Humankind has the ability to act contrary to God's plan. (See Section Two's discussion on *freedom of contradiction*.) God directs all events, and yet humans perform evil acts. If humankind did *not* have the ability to act contrary to those God-directed evil acts, then they couldn't be guilty of personal sin. Middle knowledge is the only way God could both direct the events of the world and yet not be responsible for the evil that occurs in it.

In fact, Molinism has already conceded this within the fabric of its model: Human freedom is the very thing that hinders God's desire to save all peoples, and so He could not actualize the Possible World in which all peoples are saved. However, within our Actual World (current reality), God ordered circumstances to bring about the maximum amount of saved individuals. We *could* do differently (think of the illustration in Section Two with Ashley and Manuel), but we simply *will not*. That is a crucial distinction.

—Molinism is deterministic. Some object that since God planned for individuals to do certain things, then they could not do otherwise. Therefore, individuals are on a fixed path in life and cannot do different from what God has determined them to do.

First, terms must be defined. Determinism and fatalism are different. Determinism means that causes wholly determine what someone will do and eliminates any sort of decision making. This is similar to the naturalistic claim that my actions are wholly a result of evolution, cultural influence, genetic inheritance, and so on, to say that I am not responsible for what I do. Fatalism means that the end result wholly determines what someone will do and eliminates decision making from the conversation. Through God's middle knowledge, Molinism avoids these two pitfalls and simply says that God ordains.

Second, the objection is false. Individuals are *not* on a fixed path in life. They truly *could* do differently. If they couldn't truly do differently, then they could not be guilty of sin. (See Section Two on *freedom of contradiction*.) Humans need to freely choose evil, otherwise God is responsible for it. And that requires that they be free to do otherwise. And yet God somehow needs to direct their actions. (See Section Two on all events being causally linked.) His middle knowledge seems to be the only way to do this. Molinism is not deterministic, because individuals truly *could* do differently. But God has perfect knowledge of what they *would* do and does not need to force them in any way. His middle knowledge allows Him to direct events without determining them (as defined above), and it also allows Him to reach the results He wants without falling into fatalism (as defined above). God's middle knowledge is the only way to avoid making God the author of evil while also attributing Him with the power to direct human events.

—*Molinism denies God's aseity.* Here, the objector says that since counterfactuals originate from humans, not God, then God does not have true aseity, that is, He does not exist independently. But since when do the subjects of propositions determine the dependence or independence of their possessors? Let's throw out a hypothetical proposition: In circumstances C, subject S would do action A. Let's call that Proposition 1. Now let's say I, Truett Billups, have knowledge of Proposition 1. How does the subject of that proposition determine my dependence upon the subject? In other words, how does my very existence become dependent upon the subject of the propositions I possess? The subject of a proposition determines nothing about the dependence or independence of the proposition's possessor. If the proposition is true, then it doesn't matter who possesses it, and the subject of the proposition determines nothing about the ontology of the possessor. Let's say a goldsmith makes a coin. I find the coin. My possessing the coin says nothing about my ontology. True, I would not have the coin if the goldsmith hadn't made it, but that in no way makes my very ontology and existence dependent upon the goldsmith. In the same way, the subjects that generate counterfactuals and propositions determine nothing about the ontology and existence of whoever possesses knowledge of those counterfactuals and propositions.

Molina answers this objection early in his *Concordia*. He uses the analogy of a lamp.

> For example, the fact that this lamp by which I am writing is now emitting light from itself is a contingent effect that was

able not to exist; and even though this effect proceeds by a necessity of nature from the lamp itself as from a natural cause, the source of its contingency was not the lamp, but rather the person who by his free choice lit the lamp, along with all the free causes that cooperated in the production of this oil and of the other things required for lighting the lamp.[44]

The lamp shines of its own accord, but he, Molina, lit the lamp. He uses the terms *proximate* and *primary*. So though he is not the *proximate and immediate* cause of the light, he is the *primary*, though remote, cause of the light. In the same way, God is not the proximate and immediate cause of free human actions, but He is their primary, though remote, cause.

—***Molinism denies total depravity.*** Essentially, yes. But there are different understandings of total depravity. Perhaps the most common understanding is that total depravity means that humans have a complete inability to respond to spiritual stimuli or seek God. Mankind is spiritually dead in the literal sense. Molinism denies this. Arguments are given in favor of human freedom in Section One, and what it means for mankind to be spiritually dead is discussed in Section Three, Soteriology. Total depravity might be better understood, not as wholly transforming mankind into beings that cannot do anything good nor respond to God's offer of salvation, but simply that sin has wholly permeated the universe and mankind. However, because of the Moral Law written on our hearts, all humans are able to accept God's offer of salvation. But sin's universality means that no Possible World exists where this happens; inevitably, many humans will reject God.

· · ·

—*Molinism denies salvation by grace.* On the contrary, Molinism strongly affirms salvation by grace. If God wanted, He could simply leave humanity alone in their sin. He was not required to send His Son to die, resurrect, and offer salvation to mankind. As argued in Section One, this was the only way to save mankind, but God still did not have to pursue it. Figuratively, He could walk away and leave humanity under the power of Satan. But "God so loved the world, that he gave his only Son, that whoever believes in him should not perish but have eternal life" (John 3:16). By His grace, God saves all who repent, put their faith in Him, and accept His global offer of salvation. The only reason anyone is saved is because God is all-loving and graciously saves them. See Section Three, Soteriology, for a discussion of such verses as Ephesians 2:8-9 which says, "For by grace you have been saved through faith. And this is not your own doing; it is the gift of God, not a result of works, so that no one may boast."

—*Molinism is unnecessarily complicated.* Some object, "Why couldn't God just predestine those individuals whom He foreknows will accept His offer of salvation?" That is, God foreknows which individuals will accept salvation, and He predestines them. This objection suffers from two major difficulties. First, it doesn't give God a choice. If God simply foreknows those individuals who freely accept His salvation and predestines them, then that doesn't give God a choice in salvation, nor be compatible with what the Scriptures teach. Please review the argument for predestination in Section One. Obviously, God predestines individuals somewhat apart, or in spite of, their will in order to work out His plans. He is not simply reacting to what He knows individuals will do in the future; He is also directing it in some way. Secondly, it seems to assume that God isn't free to create a different world. The world simply is, and God knows what will happen in it. This seems to challenge His omnipotence, even properly defined as *maximal power*. The objection assumes that God is not omnipotent enough to create a different world; He is stuck with the one He's got. So, this objection removes God's choice of which individuals to predestine, and it removes God's omnipotence of which world to create. If the objector responds, "Well, God probably created a world in which the most amount of people freely accept His salvation," then that sounds an awful lot like Molinism.

—God hardened Pharaoh's heart. The verse in question is Exodus 9:12 which says, "But the LORD hardened the heart of Pharaoh, and he did not listen to them, as the LORD had spoken to Moses." Doesn't this show that God can, and does, infringe upon the human will? We need not understand it as God *directly* hardening Pharaoh's heart. If we do, then we might also be compelled to understand Judas' betrayal as being *directly* caused by God. If this were the case, then Judas did not freely betray Christ and was not guilty of doing so, being denied the freedom of contradiction. But in the same way that God directed Judas to betray Christ via middle knowledge, which allows for the freedom of contradiction, He also hardened Pharaoh's heart via middle knowledge. God created Pharaoh and set him in such circumstances so that Pharaoh freely hardened his own heart and stubbornly refused to let the Israelites go. God did not *directly* harden Pharaoh's heart. Rather, God hardened it *indirectly* via middle knowledge. Also, the additional statements in Exodus that Pharaoh hardened his own heart (Exodus 8:15, 32) imply that God used some sort of indirect method. How could God harden Pharaoh's heart, yet Pharaoh harden his own heart, simultaneously? Through middle knowledge.

. . .

—God gives us understanding. This objection comes from 1 John 5:20, which says, "And we know that the Son of God has come and has given us understanding, so that we may know him who is true; and we are in him who is true, in his Son Jesus Christ. He is the true God and eternal life." Sometimes this is perceived as an objection to Molinism to argue that human freedom has no place in salvation. Objectors say that God brings understanding to our minds and our hearts through solely intrinsic means, such as the intrinsic operation of the Holy Spirit. This interpretation is false. As the passage says, it is absolutely true that "the Son of God has come and given us understanding," but this should not be interpreted as denying human freedom in salvation. God uses a variety of means to convict us and bring us understanding of His truth. Molinism extends God's resources of conviction to include both intrinsic and extrinsic means. Extrinsically, God uses the beauty and order of creation. Romans 1:20 says, "For his invisible attributes, namely, his eternal power and divine nature, have been clearly perceived, ever since the creation of the world, in the things that have been made. So they are without excuse." He uses the "things that have been made" to reveal His "invisible attributes." This extrinsic means operates upon the Moral Law to bring intrinsic conviction (Romans 2:6-16). The same is true of Jesus, the Son of God. His words of truth are the extrinsic means of bringing understanding to our minds and hearts and direct us into a state of repentance where we freely accept His global offer of salvation. 1 John 5:20 does not at all offend a Molinist understanding of providence.

. . .

—God doesn't have middle knowledge. This objection is strange. Nearly all theologians would admit that God has knowledge of everything that could or would happen in any given situation. Many biblical passages can be brought up easily to confirm this (Section Two). But the objection seems more against the term *middle knowledge* rather than the concept. Some might say, "If it isn't part of God's free knowledge, then it must be part of His natural knowledge. There is no middle knowledge." But that's like saying, "There are only fruits and vegetables. No strawberries!" There is no problem with identifying a kind of fruit as a strawberry, and there is no problem of identifying a kind of God's knowledge as middle knowledge. Again, the objection seems to be more against the jumble of letters that spell "middle knowledge" than it is against the concept itself. Some might say, "It isn't necessary to identify middle knowledge." What they mean is, "It isn't necessary *to my view of providence* to identify middle knowledge." It is, however, necessary to Molinism. And so God possesses middle knowledge, regardless of whether someone recognizes the term or not.

—God cannot have middle knowledge prior to His divine decree. This is one of the two main ones mentioned at the beginning of the section. It says that God can have knowledge of counterfactuals only *after* His divine decree to actualize a world. Prior to that, no Actual World exists to serve as a reference point for His middle knowledge.

However, objectors do not seem to fully appreciate the three logical moments of God's knowledge (Section Two). In the first moment, God knows the range of Possible Worlds and has natural knowledge. He knows everything that everyone *could* do in any given situation. In the second moment, God knows the range of Feasible Worlds and has middle knowledge.

He knows everything that everyone *would* do in any given situation. In the third moment, God knows the Actual World. He knows what everyone everything that everyone *will* do in the circumstances in which they find themselves.

I just don't see any reason to deny that God has middle knowledge prior to His divine decree. In any case, it seems exceedingly strange to think that God doesn't know what will happen in a world until He creates it! To deny God's middle knowledge prior to His divine decree seems to posit that He created the world blindly. He had no clue what was going to happen. The objection, if successful, seems to collapse into a kind of Open Theism, that God doesn't know the future. And not many Christians are willing to go there theologically.

—*True counterfactuals do not exist.* This objection is one of the two main ones mentioned at the beginning of this section. It says that counterfactuals do not have a basis in reality (they do not occur), and so do not exist. Only those events that actually occur (events in the Actual World) have a basis in reality and exist. This objection seems strange and, like I said in the introduction, a bit esoteric and speculative. Scriptural arguments can be drawn up in favor of counterfactuals (Section Two), and common experience consistently affirms their existence. Counterfactuals simply entertain the possibility that the world *could* have been different. If so, then different events *would* occur! It is at this point that skeptics and proponents of middle knowledge mostly talk in circles.

—*Why not leave these things a mystery?* If we accept this objection, then why not leave *everything* about God a mystery? Why bother answering *any* theological questions? The aim of theology is to understand the mind and ways of God as best we can. If that isn't our aim, then we might as well close the seminaries and shrug our shoulders. It's fine, at the end of the day, with a cup of coffee in our hands, to admit that we probably don't know very much about God. But while we're doing theology—writing books, giving presentations, and discussing things—the whole aim is to answer questions. So it seems that this objection is not against Molinism in particular. Rather, it challenges the whole project of theology.

—If Molinism is so great, then why isn't it more popular? Molinism doesn't make much sense unless it's presented all at once, as one cohesive model. Molinist books and articles often argue one point of Molinism, answer one objection, or apply it to one doctrine. But so far, I have not yet encountered a resource which presents it all at once, links causally-determined free agents to logical impossibilities, gives specific illustrations (such as Ashley and Manuel), applies it to a variety of doctrines, and answers popular-level objections. Thus, this book. Also, people often get scared away by its use of unfamiliar terms such as middle knowledge, feasible worlds, counterfactuals, etc. Straightaway, the model sounds unbiblical. So, we can find a variety of understandable reasons why Molinism isn't popular. Perhaps that will change.

Conclusion

Molinism boldly claims to resolve many thorny theological paradoxes. God is omniscient, omnipotent, and omnibenevolent. He desires the salvation of all peoples, yet most are lost. Humans are free agents, yet God sovereignly predestines. The Bible is the Word of God, yet contains human elements. God directs the events of the world, yet we cocreate the world with our prayers. (In saying "cocreate," we do not lift mankind to equality with God, for He determines which prayers to answer and which not to.) God predestines individuals and saves them by His grace, yet part of that responsibility is laid on our evangelistic efforts. Molinism answers all of these paradoxes by saying God directs the events of the world by knowing what every individual *would* do in any given circumstance and arranging things to bring about the maximum amount of saved individuals.

Imposing logical boundaries upon the power of the Godhead and positing the inevitability of evil might sound repulsive to many Christians. Yet this seems consistent with God's love for the whole world, His desire to save all peoples, His grief over sin, His plea for peoples to repent, the power of evil, spiritual warfare, human freedom, and Christ's fear of approaching the cross but knowing that it's the only to save humanity (Matthew 26:36-46). The logical boundaries are philosophically sound and Scripturally supported.

Molinism is not, as I've heard the critique, "anthropocentric," with a rabid desire to protect human freedom. Rather, it desires to protect God's omnibenevolence. If God is all-loving, then why does evil exist and why isn't everyone saved? Perhaps evil is the inevitable result of creating humans in the *imago dei* who can truly "choose this day whom [they] will serve" (Joshua 24:15). The seemingly incompatibility of an omnibenevolent deity coexisting with an evil universe, combined with Scriptural passages supporting human freedom, give us reason to think that the problem of evil may not need to be thrown into the theological territory of inscrutability. Perhaps God's omnipotence should be properly understood as having maximal power rather than being able to do *anything*. In any case, even if God were not omnipotent, then it might not be ideal, but not all is lost. We would still have the comfort of knowing that the most powerful being that exists is on our side. But if God were not omnibenevolent, then that would be truly devastating, for we would be utterly without hope. Thankfully, that is not the case. God does everything out of love.

I would say it a thousand times: Molinism is only a model. It would be wrong (both factually and morally) for anyone to claim that the Bible itself teaches any particular model of divine providence. Aside from core orthodox beliefs, we must hold our theological concepts loosely. We may think that one particular model of providence is best, but we must still respect and politely dialogue with Christians who believe differently. As the pietists said, "In essentials, unity. In nonessentials, liberty. In all things, charity." Let's keep this wise saying in mind whenever we attempt to plunge the depths of God.

Appendix A
PAUL AND GREEK PHILOSOPHY

Paul was born into a devout Jewish family as a Roman citizen. While young, he was sent to receive education at the school of Gamaliel, a famous rabbi (Acts 22:3). The school was notable for its balanced education, likely giving Paul broad exposure to classical literature.

Perhaps unknown to many Christians, Paul draws heavily from Greek philosophy throughout his letters. He uses terms, metaphors, and direct quotes in order to communicate and argue his theological points. By using philosophy to bring clarity to theology, Molinism is consistent with a Pauline way of thinking. The following is a list of some of his known references and quotes.

1 Corinthians 9:16b—For necessity is laid upon me. Woe to me if I do not preach the gospel!

Plato writes, "But necessity was laid upon me—the word of God I thought ought to be considered first." (Dialogues, *Apology*)

1 Corinthians 9:24a—Do you not know that in a race all the runners run, but only one receives the prize?

Plato writes, "But such as are true racers, arriving at the end, both receive the prizes and are crowned." (*Republic*, Book X)

1 Corinthians 12:14-17—For the body does not consist of one member but of many. If the foot should say, "Because I am not a hand, I do not belong to the body," that would not make it any less a part of the body. And if the ear should say, "Because I am not an eye, I do not belong to the body," that would not make it any less a part of the body. If the whole body were an eye, where would be the sense of hearing? If the whole body were an ear, where would be the sense of smell?

Plato writes for Socrates, "Is virtue a single whole, and are justice and self-control and holiness parts of it? ... as the parts of a face are parts-mouth, nose, eyes and ears." Socrates then probes into the metaphor further by asking Protagoras if they agree that each part serves a different purpose, just as the features of a face do, and the parts make the whole, but each serves a different purpose—"the eye is not like the ear nor has it the same function." (Dialogues, *Protagoras*)

1 Corinthians 12:25-26—That there may be no division in the body, but that the members may have the same care for one another. If one member suffers, all suffer together; if one member is honored, all rejoice together.

Plato writes for Socrates, "whose state is most like that of an individual man. For example, if the finger of one of us is wounded, the entire community of bodily connections stretching to the soul for 'integration' with the dominant part is made aware, and all of it feels the pain as a whole." (Dialogues, *Protagoras*)

1 Corinthians 13:12a—For now we see in a mirror dimly, but then face to face.

Plato writes, "I am very far from admitting that he who contemplates existences through the medium of thought, sees them only 'through a glass, darkly,' anymore than he who sees them in their working effects." (Dialogues, *Phaedo*)

1 Corinthians 15:33—Do not be deceived: "Bad company ruins good morals."

This is an iambic line from *Thasis* of Menander, who probably quoted a play by Euripides.

Acts 17:24—The God who made the world and everything in it, being Lord of heaven and earth, does not live in temples made by man.

Euripides said, "What house built by craftsmen could enclose the form divine within enfolding walls?" (Lucian, *Sacr.* 11)

Acts 17:26-27—And he made from one man every nation of mankind to live on all the face of the earth, having determined allotted periods and the boundaries of their dwelling place, that they should seek God, and perhaps feel their way toward him and find him. Yet he is actually not far from each one of us….

Seneca, a Greek Stoic, wrote, "God is near you, he is with you, he is within you."

Acts 17:28—As even some of your own poets have said, "For we are indeed his offspring."

Quote from *Phaenomena* by Aratus.

Acts 17:29—Being then God's offspring, we ought not to think that the divine being is like gold or silver or stone, an image formed by the art and imagination of man.

Seneca wrote, "Thou shalt not form him of silver and gold: a true likeness of God cannot be molded of this material."

Galatians 5:23b—Against such things there is no law.

Romans 2:14—For when Gentiles, who do not have the law, by nature do what the law requires, they are a law to themselves, even though they do not have the law.

Allusions to Aristotle, who wrote of wisdom and virtue that, "Against such there is no law, for they themselves are a law." (*Politics*, 350 BC)

Romans 7:22-23—For I delight in the law of God, in my inner being, but I see in my members another law waging war against the law of my mind and making me captive to the law of sin that dwells in my members.

Plato writes, "There is a victory and defeat—the first and best of victories, the lowest and worst of defeats—which each man gains or sustains at the hands not of another, but of himself; this shows that there is a war against ourselves—going on in every individual of us." (*Laws*, Book 1)

Romans 12:4—For as in one body we have many members, and the members do not all have the same function....

Allusion to Socrates, who wrote, "To begin with, our several natures are not all alike but different. One man is naturally fitted for one task, and another for another."

Philippians 1:21—For to me to live is Christ, and to die is gain.

Plato writes, "Now if death is like this, I say that to die is gain." (Dialogues, *Apology*)

1 Thessalonians 5:15—See that no one repays anyone evil for evil, but always seek to do good to one another and to everyone.

Plato writes, "Then we ought not to retaliate or render evil for evil to anyone, whatever evil we may have suffered from him." (Dialogues, *Crito*)

Appendix B
THE VALUE OF APOLOGETICS

Since the human will plays a role in salvation, then how does that change the way we evangelize? We start valuing apologetics. When I say apologetics, most people think of defending the Christian faith with reason and evidence. It means arguing on secular ground that Christianity is a rationally defensible viewpoint. Your arguments do not assume the truth of Christianity from the outset, but that's where they conclude. This is called *classical apologetics*.

However, not everyone understands apologetics in that way. There is another method called *presuppositional apologetics*. It finds its roots in the work of 20th century Dutch theologian Cornelius Van Til. He viewed unsaved people as being spiritually dead in the literal sense and, as a result, completely unable to think rationally. Consider verses such as Ephesians 4:18, which reads, "They are darkened in their understanding, alienated from the life of God because of the ignorance that is in them due to the hardness of their hearts."[45] For Van Til, this means that reason and evidence are doomed to fail. And so, as Christians, our job is simply to preach the Gospel, because that is what redeems a person's soul—not cleverly devised argumentation.

I disagree for a few reasons. The first reason being that, even though argumentation does not save a person's soul, neither does preaching the Gospel. The work of the Holy Spirit is the only thing that saves a person's soul. And yet: We are called to evangelize, because God works through our evangelistic efforts to save people by His grace.

When I say apologetics, I mean classical apologetics. So, let's look at four reasons why apologetics is important, even necessary, for Christians to study. The first reason is this: Apologetics is for making disciples. Some people might take the presuppositional approach and object, "All you need is the Gospel! Just tell people the Gospel and let the Holy Spirit do the work!" The problem with this attitude is that it can be used to excuse Christians from doing anything. "Don't spend so much time trying to raise your children yourselves, just bring them to church and let the Holy Spirit work in their lives. Don't spend so much effort trying to defeat sin in your life, just pray and let the Holy Spirit work it out." The Holy Spirit does, in fact, work in the world and in people's lives, but this does not excuse the Christian believer from taking action. This applies to evangelism. The Christian believer is obligated to use every tool at his disposal to convert unbelievers. Frankly, anything else is laziness.

Other people might object to this, saying, "People are not won to Christ through arguments, but rather through love or the working of the Holy Spirit." This is simply false. Many people have converted to Christ simply because they heard a good argument. One example is C.S. Lewis. He was once an atheist and became a Christian because his close friend J.R.R. Tolkien presented good reasons for Christianity. William Lane Craig, often looked at as the foremost Christian apologist in the world, says this: "I think that those who believe that apologetics is not effective in evangelism just frankly haven't done enough evangelism."[46] Once you start doing evangelism, once you start talking with unbelievers who have serious questions regarding the existence of God and the reliability of the Bible, you find out, very quickly, just how useful classical apologetics really is.

And anyway, notice the wording of this point: To make disciples. We are not called to save anyone, that's God's job. Our job is simply to teach people the Gospel and make disciples. And, as evidenced by Judas, you don't have to be saved to be a disciple of Christ.

Let's look at some scriptural support for this point. We'll consider a few passages. The first is Acts 17:1-4, which says,

> Now when they [Paul and Silas] had passed through Amphipolis and Apollonia, they came to Thessalonica, where there was a synagogue of the Jews. And Paul went in, as was his custom, and on three Sabbath days he reasoned with them from the Scriptures, explaining and proving that it was necessary for the Christ to suffer and to rise from the dead, and saying, "This Jesus, whom I proclaim to you, is the Christ." And some of them were persuaded and joined Paul and Silas, as did a great many of the devout Greeks and not a few of the leading women.

Here we have Paul making it a habit to argue with people that Christ rose from the dead. Now, you have to remember, at this point in history the New Testament had not been written nor canonized. Paul is arguing for Christ's resurrection apart from explicit statements in Scripture.

Our second passage comes from later in that same chapter, 17:22-31. Here we have Paul arguing for the authority of God and the resurrection of Christ, starting with the pagan idol to the unknown God. He even quotes pagan philosophers and pagan mythologies to support his point. Paul uses every tool at his disposal to convince people of the truth of the Gospel.

Our third passage comes from Acts as well. Paul is on a roll, it seems.

> And he [Paul] entered the synagogue and for three months spoke boldly, reasoning and persuading them about the kingdom of God. But when some became stubborn and continued in unbelief, speaking evil of the Way before the congregation, he withdrew from them and took the disciples with him, reasoning daily in the hall of Tyrannus. This continued for two years, so that all the residents of Asia heard the word of the Lord, both Jews and Greeks. (Acts 19:8-10)

And then, Acts 28:23-24.

> When they had appointed a day for him [Paul], they came to him at his lodging in greater numbers. From morning till evening he expounded to them, testifying to the kingdom of God and trying to convince them about Jesus both from the Law of Moses and from the Prophets. And some were convinced by what he said, but others disbelieved.

There is absolutely a place for arguing and trying to convince people. It isn't enough to simply repeat a three or four-point Gospel presentation to someone. If that's all you have time for, fine. But you should engage in more than that, if you are able. Paul started with what people already accepted to be true—whether that be the Old Testament Scriptures or pagan mythologies—and then argued from there to the truth of the Gospel.

Our final passage comes from Jesus himself in John 10:38-

39. Jesus is speaking with the Jews and they accuse him of blaspheming. He responds, "If I am not doing the works of my Father, then do not believe me; but if I do them, even though you do not believe me, believe the works, that you may know and understand that the Father is in me and I am in the Father." Jesus is saying, "Fine if you won't believe me when I say I'm the Son of God, then I'll prove it to you by what I do," presumably miracles or some such thing. You have to understand he was making incredibly radical claims. I think anyone would be skeptical of someone who claimed to be God. And yet, Jesus doesn't just leave people hanging when they don't believe him. He invited critique and verification.

And just to deflect the idea that non-Christians can't think rationally, let's consider just briefly one passage before we move on to our second point. Romans 2:12:-16,

> For all who have sinned without the law will also perish without the law, and all who have sinned under the law will be judged by the law. For it is not the hearers of the law who are righteous before God, but the doers of the law who will be justified. For when Gentiles, who do not have the law, by nature do what the law requires, they are a law to themselves, even though they do not have the law. They show that the work of the law is written on their hearts, while their conscience also bears witness, and their conflicting thoughts accuse or even excuse them on that day when, according to my gospel, God judges the secrets of men by Christ Jesus.

Here Paul says, in no uncertain terms, that unbelievers—Gentiles—have a conscience and know God's law "by nature." And so, classical apologetics is not shouting a message to a deaf man, but rather reasoning with someone who has retained his God-given rational, and even moral, faculties.

The second reason for apologetics is this: Apologetics is for strengthening believers. For Christians who have never doubted their faith, apologetics can give them courage and confidence. It might even give them the confidence they need to evangelize.

But for Christians who do doubt their faith, apologetics can help answer questions and keep them committed to Christ. Does the fact that a Christian is doubting his beliefs mean that he is a lesser Christian? Absolutely not! We're talking about the direction and conviction of our lives and possibly eternity. Aren't you interested in whether your beliefs are true or not? Someone might study and read and evaluate which car is best to buy, but when it comes to whether God exists or whether Christ actually rose from the dead they're just going to shrug and say, "I know it in my heart"? Christian beliefs are far more important than buying a car, and so we need to put far more effort into determining whether we should be committed to them or not.

Let's consider scriptural support for this point. The point is this: At least two books of our New Testament were written for the sole purpose of apologetics to strengthen the faith of believers. Those books are Luke and Acts. Acts is unanimously considered to be the sequel to Luke. Here is the introduction to Acts, verses 1-3.

> In the first book, O Theophilus, I have dealt with all that Jesus began to do and teach, until the day when he was taken up, after he had given commands through the Holy Spirit to the apostles whom he had chosen. He presented himself alive to them after his suffering by many proofs, appearing to them during forty days and speaking about the kingdom of God.

That first book was Luke, which was also addressed to

Theophilus. Let's look at the introduction to Luke which essentially sets the tone for Acts as well. Luke 1:1-4.

> Inasmuch as many have undertaken to compile a narrative of the things that have been accomplished among us, just as those who from the beginning were eyewitnesses and ministers of the word have delivered them to us, it seemed good to me also, having followed all things closely for some time past, to write an orderly account for you, most excellent Theophilus, that you may have certainty concerning the things you have been taught.

Like Jesus, Luke invites critique and investigation. He doesn't have a problem defending the rationality of the Gospel by compiling an evidence-based historical narrative. The purpose of his book, explicitly stated, is to give believers certainty in the face of doubt. And so we can conclude that at least two books of our New Testament, Luke and Acts, were written for the explicit purpose of classical apologetics. Argumentation and reasoning in evangelism were not only acceptable in the time of Jesus and the early church, it was common.

The third reason for apologetics is this: Apologetics justifies religious liberty. If you want a safe, moral environment in which to raise your children, then culture needs to respect your beliefs. If you can't give a rational defense for your beliefs, then society will simply think you're crazy. Society doesn't allow crazy people very many rights. If society deems that you are psychologically unfit, then the consequences could include taking your children from your care and giving them to someone else to raise, putting you in a mental health facility, and criminalizing religious convictions. These might seem like extreme examples, but they are not unheard of.

Here is a quote from the famous atheistic philosopher Karl Marx. He says,

> The abolition of religion as the illusory happiness of the people is the demand for their real happiness. To call on them to give up their illusions about their condition is to call on them to give up a condition that requires illusions.[47]

Are your religious beliefs illusions? Should they be abolished, even against your will, to make you and the rest of society truly happy?

Here's another quote by a contemporary atheist named Sam Harris,

> We have names for people who have many beliefs for which there is no rational justification. When their beliefs are extremely common we call them 'religious'; otherwise they are likely to be called 'mad', 'psychotic' or 'delusional'.... Clearly there is sanity in numbers. And yet, it is merely an accident of history that it is considered normal in our society to believe that the Creator of the universe can hear your thoughts, while it is demonstrative of mental illness to believe that he is communicating with you by having the rain tap in Morse code on your bedroom window. And so, while religious people are not generally mad, their core beliefs absolutely are.[48]

Statements like these are why you need to be able to present your beliefs in a rational way that society will respect. Otherwise, people will think that you are getting in the way of society's wellbeing, and you risk losing your religious liberty.

Finally: Apologetics fulfills the Greatest Commandment. In

Matthew (22:37), Mark (12:30), and Luke (10:27)—all of the Synoptic Gospels—Jesus is recorded telling us the Greatest Commandment. Let's read from Mark,

> "And one of the scribes came up and heard them disputing with one another, and seeing that he answered them well, asked him, "Which commandment is the most important of all?" Jesus answered, "The most important is, 'Hear, O Israel: The Lord our God, the Lord is one. And you shall love the Lord your God with all your heart and with all your soul and with all your mind and with all your strength.' The second is this: 'You shall love your neighbor as yourself.' There is no other commandment greater than these." (Mark 12:28-31)

Jesus is quoting from Deuteronomy 6:5 in which Yahweh Himself tells Israel the Greatest Commandment. Yet Jesus doesn't quote it perfectly. He actually adds the word *mind*. I find that very interesting. So Yahweh says to love the Lord your God with all your heart, soul, and strength, and yet Jesus adds the word *mind*.

So we're supposed to love the Lord our God with all our heart, soul, mind, and strength, for what purpose? Well, what better place can we turn to than Jesus' final command to the disciples at His Ascension. Matthew 28:16-20,

> Now the eleven disciples went to Galilee, to the mountain to which Jesus had directed them. And when they saw him they worshiped him, but some doubted. And Jesus came and said to them, "All authority in heaven and on earth has been given to me. Go therefore and make disciples of all nations, baptizing them in the name of the Father and of the Son and of

the Holy Spirit, teaching them to observe all that I have commanded you. And behold, I am with you always, to the end of the age.

Our main job is to make disciples, to convert unbelievers. As we've seen, classical evidence-based apologetics is an effective way of doing that. It was Paul's preferred method of evangelism, Jesus invited such critique and validation, and two whole books of our New Testament were written for the explicit purpose of classical evidence-based apologetics. If it works, then at the very least Christians are obligated to encourage it. If we are not doing everything we can to fulfill the Great Commission, then we are in danger of violating the Greatest Commandment. Charles Spurgeon described this attitude very well. He said, "If sinners be damned, at least let them leap to Hell over our dead bodies." The alternative is simply laziness which is, as I said, a violation of the Greatest Commandment.

So, to summarize the four purposes of Classical Apologetics: 1) Apologetics is for converting unbelievers, and we looked at scriptural support from the ministries of Paul and Jesus. 2) Apologetics is for strengthening believers, and we looked at scriptural support from Luke and Acts. 3) Apologetics justifies religious liberty, and we looked at a possible secular reaction to a religious faith that is unsubstantiated with evidence and argumentation. 4) Apologetics fulfills the Greatest Commandment, and we looked at support from the Great Commission. Since human freedom plays a role in salvation, then so does argument, persuasion, and classical apologetics.

Endnotes

1. Spurgeon, C. H. Quoted in Packer, J. I. 1973. *Knowing God.* London: Hodder & Stoughton, 13-14.

2. Other verses that refer to God's omnipotence: Genesis 17:1, 18:14; Revelation 19:6; Psalm 33:9; Jeremiah 32:17; Job 42:1-2; Matthew 19:26.

3. Discussions get complicated, but William Lane Craig defines omnipotence this way: God can bring about any state of affairs which is logically possible for anyone to bring about in that situation. (Craig, W. Defenders 3, Doctrine of God, Part 16. Reasonable Faith. Posted on reasonablefaith.com.)

4. Molina, L. *Concordia IV.* ed. Alfred J. Freddoso. Ithaca, NY: Cornell University Press, 202.

5. Molina, L. *Concordia IV.* ed. Alfred J. Freddoso. Ithaca, NY: Cornell University Press, 182.

6. Carson, D.A. 2002. *Divine Sovereignty and Human Responsibility:*

Biblical Perspectives in Tension. Eugene, OR: Wipf and Stock Pub, 18-22.

7. Causal Determinism: Causes outside of humanity's control wholly determine what they do.

8. Causal Determinism: Causes outside of humanity's control wholly determine what they do.

9. Molina, L. *Concordia IV.* ed. Alfred J. Freddoso. Ithaca, NY: Cornell University Press, 168.

10. Molina, L. *Concordia IV.* ed. Alfred J. Freddoso. Ithaca, NY: Cornell University Press, 117. Molina refers to this passage using the Vulgate title 1 Kings 23:10-12.

11. Some readers might think, "But you said God could do anything logically possible. This means He can actualize any Possible World He wants, including the one where all individuals freely accept Him." This objection is astute, but it fails. Possible Worlds are those which have not yet accounted for human freedom. After accounting for human freedom, some of those worlds become impossible while others remain possible. However, Molinism uses the terms *infeasible* and *feasible* to make clear that we have now accounted for human freedom.

12. Craig, W. 1999. *The Only Wise God.* Eugene, OR: Wipf and Stock Publishers, 127.

13. Craig, W. 1999. *The Only Wise God.* Eugene, OR: Wipf and Stock Publishers, 131.

14. Causal Determinism: Causes outside of humanity's control wholly determine what they do.

15. Craig, W. Molinism vs. Calvinism. Reasonable Faith. Posted on reasonablefaith.com April 18, 2010, accessed October 11, 2017.

16. Molina, L. *Concordia IV*. ed. Alfred J. Freddoso. Ithaca, NY: Cornell University Press, 223.

17. Molina, L. *Concordia IV*. ed. Alfred J. Freddoso. Ithaca, NY: Cornell University Press, 224-225.

18. Hasker, W. 1990. Response to Thomas Flint. *Philosophical Studies*. 60 (1/2): 117-118.

19. Craig, W. 'No Other Name': A Middle Knowledge Perspective on the Exclusivity of Salvation through Christ. *Faith and Philosophy*. 6 (1989): 172-188.

20. Craig, W. 'Lest Anyone Should Fall': A Middle Knowledge Perspective on Perseverance and Apostolic Warnings. *International Journal for Philosophy of Religion*. 29 (1991): 65-74.

21. Craig, W. 'Men Moved by the Holy Spirit Spoke from God' (2 Peter 1:2): A Middle Knowledge Perspective on Biblical Inspiration. *Philosophia Christi*. 1 (1999): 45-82.

22. Flint, T. Middle Knowledge and the Doctrine of Infallibility. *Philosophical Perspectives*, vol. 5, *Philosophy of Religion*, ed. James E Tomberlin (Atascadero, CA: Ridgeview, 1991), 373-393.

23. Flint, T. 'A Death He Freely Accepted': Molinist Reflections on the Incarnation. *Faith and Philosophy*. 18 (2001): 3-20.

24. Unwittingly by Dembski, W. 2009. *The End of Christianity*. Nashville: Broadman & Holman.

25. Craig, W. Divine Sovereignty and Quantum Indeterminism. Reasonable Faith. Posted on reasonablefaith.com December 7, 2009, accessed October 10, 2017.

26. Craig, W. Molinism: Middle Knowledge and Divine Election. Reasonable Faith. Posted on reasonablefaith.com October 19, 2008, accessed October 11, 2017.

27. Craig. W. Defenders 2, Doctrine of Man, Part 10. Reasonable Faith. Posted on reasonablefaith.com.

28. Romans 7:7 says, "Yet if it had not been for the law, I would not have known sin. For I would not have known what it is to covet if the law had not said, 'You shall not covet.'" This verse might be understood as a pair of counterfactuals regarding the extrinsic operation of the mosaic law on Paul's heart. It is similar to the counterfactual of John 15:22 where Jesus says, "If I had not come and spoken to them, they would not have been guilty of sin, but now they have no excuse for their sin."

29. MacGregor, K. 2015. *Luis de Molina: The Life and Theology of the Founder of Middle Knowledge*. Grand Rapids, MI: Zondervan, 106.

30. Possible objections to what I'm saying include 1 Corinthians 15:27 and Ephesians 1:20-23.

31. Wenham, J. 2009. *Christ and the Bible*, 3rd edition. Eugene, OR: Wipf and Stock Publishers, 17-18.

32. Wenham, J. 2009. *Christ and the Bible*, 3rd edition. Eugene, OR: Wipf and Stock Publishers, 17.

33. Warfield, B. 1970. "The Biblical Idea of Inspiration," in *The Inspiration and Authority of the Bible*, ed. Samuel G. Craig with an Intro. by Cornelius Van Til. Philadelphia: Presbyterian & Reformed, 154-155.

34. Craig, W. 'Lest Anyone Should Fall': A Middle Knowledge Perspective on Perseverance and Apostolic Warnings. *International Journal for Philosophy of Religion*. 29 (1991): 65-74.

35. MacGregor, K. 2015. *Luis de Molina: The Life and Theology of the Founder of Middle Knowledge*. Grand Rapids, MI: Zondervan, 124-125.

36. MacGregor, K. 2015. *Luis de Molina: The Life and Theology of the Founder of Middle Knowledge*. Grand Rapids, MI: Zondervan, 125.

37. MacGregor, K. 2015. *Luis de Molina: The Life and Theology of the Founder of Middle Knowledge*. Grand Rapids, MI: Zondervan, 125-126.

38. MacGregor, K. 2015. *Luis de Molina: The Life and Theology of the Founder of Middle Knowledge*. Grand Rapids, MI: Zondervan, 127-128.

39. MacGregor, K. 2015. *Luis de Molina: The Life and Theology of the Founder of Middle Knowledge*. Grand Rapids, MI: Zondervan, 130.

40. Perszyk, K. 2011. Introduction, in *Molinism: The Contemporary Debate*. Perszyk, K. ed. NY: Oxford University Press, 7.

41. MacGregor, K. 2015. *Luis de Molina: The Life and Theology of*

the Founder of Middle Knowledge. Grand Rapids, MI: Zondervan, 104.

42. Molina, L. *Concordia IV.* ed. Alfred J. Freddoso. Ithaca, NY: Cornell University Press, 181-183.

43. Molina, L. *Concordia IV.* ed. Alfred J. Freddoso. Ithaca, NY: Cornell University Press, 184.

44. Molina, L. *Concordia IV.* ed. Alfred J. Freddoso. Ithaca, NY: Cornell University Press, 95.

45. A Molinist would say that even though unbelievers are darkened in their understanding, they are not wholly without light.

46. Craig, W. Defenders 2, Foundations of Christian Doctrine, Part 2. Reasonable Faith. Posted on reasonablefaith.com.

47. Marx, K. *The Communist Manifesto.*

48. Harris, S. 2005. *The End of Faith.* W.W. Norton, 22.